The Speakers Journey

Amplifying Your Voice

The Speakers Index

by Sharon Brown

Published by The Book Chief Publishing House 2022
(a trademark under Lydian Group Ltd)
Suite 2A, Blackthorn House, St Paul's Square, Birmingham, B3 1RL
www.thebookchief.com

Book Cover Design: Deearo Marketing
Editing / Typesetting / Proofreading: Sharon Brown
Publishing: Sharon Brown

THE BOOK CHIEF

IGNITE YOUR WRITING

Table of Contents

Dedication

To everyone who has taken the steps to share their valuable message with the world in the hope that it will help and guide another soul.

Foreword

By John Reed

It gives me the utmost pleasure to introduce The Speakers Index to you, a platform that fills a space in the arena that I know so well, that of Public Speaking.

There are many sides to the marketplace, but the two main areas we recognise are the supplier, namely the speakers themselves, and the purchaser, the audience. Of course, the market separates into many sectors, both public and private, but whatever the industry, how both sides meet is sometimes a little unclear.

The Speakers Index solves this problem by acting as a marketplace where all sides can meet, make their initial enquiries, and then move on to contract with the very best that is available at the time.

Competition ensures value, but more to the point, the marketplace allows both sides to engage in a successful presentation. The result satisfaction is guaranteed.

Uniquely in this sector, availability, subject knowledge, experience, and charges are known before signing the contract. All sides are protected, and the result is for the benefit of all concerned.

I would recommend The Speakers Index to anyone seeking speakers of the highest quality and standing and speakers who have demonstrable skills to share.

Acknowledgements

Thank you to all of the Contributing Authors who have taken the steps to share their stories and bring this book to life. Philip Horrod, Sue Curr, John Reed, Ellie LaCrosse, Abbi Head, Angela Roth, Ian Llewellyn-Nash, Sofia Nordgren, Sam Dossa, Mildred D. Muhammad, Nikie Piper, Jose Luis Ucar, Ritu Sharma, Jeanne Zierhoffer, Jamie Wallace.

Introduction

The aim of this book is to share the Authors journeys into the public speaking arena.

These stories are heartfelt and at times heartbreaking but with the shared outcome that all who have fought through their adversities, took the path to share their knowledge and experience with their audience in order to give something back.

Public Speaking is a fear for many (Glossophobia), and is actually the most common fear in people across the world. These Authors demonstrate that no matter how much it is feared, it can be overcome.

Once you step into your fear and out of your comfort zone, it can be one of the most empowering experiences of all.

CHAPTER 1

Those who need this, will be listening

By Abbi Head

"Why can't you look at me? Have you got something to hide?" I used to hear this a lot.

I could barely make eye contact as a child, I still consider myself an introvert, so I have become an accidental public speaker. I have gone from looking down to engaging the attention of an in-person audience of 160 with additional online attendees in my last hybrid talk.

Speaking up and standing out is something that I highly recommend to my clients. It is an essential aspect of our personal brands as business owners. People need the "know, like, and trust" factor, and public speaking delivers that with authority. What better way to get to know and connect with someone than to hear them speak?

10-minute speaking slots at networking events have allowed me to offer massive value, develop personal credibility and attract potential clients. I soon realised that going live in a social media group with thousands of fellow members would sky-rocket my confidence and self-esteem. As I have previously appeared in promotional videos, my experience has culminated in my own YouTube course modules.

In 2019 I was asked to speak at an event about Kickstarter crowdfunding by the Coventry and Warwickshire Local Enterprise Partnership, CWLEP. This event was life-changing and forged the steel heart of a new public speaker as I stood that day in front of an audience of perhaps 30; like a rabbit, in headlights, a feeling of pride suddenly washed over me. I felt overwhelmed, "Look at all these people listening to me." I thought. Now I wonder, "Who do those people need to be? Who is that one person that needs to hear what I have to say?"

That thought of sharing something engaging and compelling drives me to speak today.

Back then, I stood with my notes in my hand on that stage as my palms perspired. The paper began to crumple with moisture, and I discarded it with an uncomfortable feeling. Suddenly I was transported back to when I was very young and was asked to give a reading on stage in school. As I stood in front of my teacher when she first insisted I present in front of the school, she noticed my nerves. The paper in my hand was sodden. "I can't give you paper to hold without you making a mess of it," she said. Harsh, but true.

Fast forward to 2019 in front of my audience, that specific memory distracting me. I discarded the notes on the lectern and spoke impromptu. I lost my planned structure and have no memory of what I said to this day. All I knew was that I could not talk with notes in my hand. I was even more nervous as I had seen the leaflet for the event which described me as a "local expert". Despite everything being a complete blur, I must have nailed it. Based on that first talk, I was asked to do a similar talk for the Chamber of Commerce.

This time I was more confident. I could hide behind an impressive PowerPoint presentation.

I had combatted my fear of holding notes by making bullet points on paper and printing out my slide deck. Before the talk, I spoke with the attendees. I was surprised to find that one gentleman had come to this particular talk to hear me speak. Slightly unnerving, yet at the time, Kickstarter crowdfunding was something that few business people were using. On this occasion, I was fortunate that someone else controlled the projector and transitioned the slides.

2020 was a life-changing turn for all of us. The effects of the pandemic meant that the UK was in lockdown, and it had driven us all online. Unstable Wi-Fi connections became a curse for speaking engagements on Zoom. Working from home meant distractions and interruptions.

I was frustrated by audio Zoom-bombing during my networking talks from maintenance workers, a nearby lawnmower, energy suppliers and delivery men. Needing uninterrupted Wi-Fi also means that my partner cannot use the internet - just in case every little helps boost the signal.

Despite delivering many 10-15 minute presentations, I still had no intentions to call myself a public speaker.

Then I met a Welshman on a mission at a networking event, and my trajectory changed forever. I was invited to join one of his Toastmasters International club meetings online. Newport, Gwent was my hometown for several years when I was at art college, so my visit was like coming home. I attended and was hooked!

Not long after joining Toastmasters, I became a member of a women's academy to boost my personal brand. This incredible group of women supported each other every step of the way through lockdown and then on to the stage as the restrictions began to lift. This was a place where I could explore my topics for my educational and inspirational talks. I began to experiment by talking about snippets of my life journey, which I had never spoken about before. I began to gain the confidence to present at educational talks and networking events. I progressed to deliver a keynote speech about my own personal journey at an Awards Event with a face to face audience.

Being asked to speak at events is a privilege and a form of endorsement. Public speaking is a great way to effectively represent your own business and elevate you above your competition.

The combination of learning speech structure and evaluation, mastering a sense of timing and impromptu talks meant that I was better prepared for an interview on Ticker News in 2021. I was given 6 to 7 minutes to talk about my course entitled 'Business Planning for Creative Thinkers.' I could feel the time ticking. The experience of appearing live in front of an audience in Australia and Singapore ran smoothly as I relaxed at the notion of being asked a question I was not prepared for.

The video link failed during my second interview with the Ticker News channel. However, because of my determination and speaking experience, I was able to turn that technical malfunction into an example to others.

It is a part of my own Public Relations experience that helps me walk the talk and show my customers what can be done in these circumstances.

The way a speaker bounces back when we are thrown a curveball is crucial because it reflects personal brand and business.

One of the things that I have learned through speaking publicly is that no matter how anxious I feel, no one can tell in the audience. My internal dilemma is like a duck paddling in water but cannot be seen. Only my body and my voice show up, and I can see myself in recordings delivering with authority despite my nerves.

Another reason I feel more at ease with my content because I will research everything to make sure that I am telling the truth as far as I know. Giving an educational talk is a responsibility for the speaker to offer value and information that will serve others. I have to be factual and precise.

As Little PR Rock Marketing, my talks include many subjects, including my 5 Key ROI Marketing Principles. These include Respect, Recognition, Resilience, Reputation and Reinforcement, with each one a Return On Investment (ROI).

This is my core message. I think it's important as a speaker to have a unique perspective that makes you memorable. Therefore, intellectual property is like gold dust.

I particularly enjoy opportunities where I have a schedule of things I need to say because I like to link subjects that would otherwise seem unrelated. Finding that connection helped me when I was on the local radio talking about my course. When I listened back, I had to admit how appealing laughter can be in an interview.

I use all this experience to help my clients present themselves in webinars and presentations. As a speaker on Zoom, I often appear in the corner of the screen with a compelling slide deck behind me. I am thrilled by the responses that I have had about my online talks for both content and technicality.

"Your speech was excellent, and I love how you popped out in your presentation down the bottom - might I ask how you do that, please? That was super cool and was the best presentation I have seen in a long time (And I see them every day) - Elissa.

"Abbi, you are one brave lady!! your story is heartbreaking, but truly one of resilience, and I was in awe of how calmly and brilliantly you told it." - Jackie

When I began to speak about my journey, I soon realised that it was where I was meant to be, and it felt more like a calling than a desire. Talking about some of my experiences has given me a voice to help others. I was once a Community Mental Health Worker, and it was challenging to work one-to-one.

However, I can work one-too-many as a speaker and still get results.

I enjoy educational talks with tips and tricks to help others master their public relations and marketing. Becoming a better speaker has helped me with written content creation, including pitching to the press, blogs, social media posts, and becoming a published co-author. Finding my voice means a more robust presence online, both in person and in my digital marketing. This is what I want for my clients.

I am aware that there are times when I will speak to a younger audience and will tailor my material accordingly. I use my 'Pantomime Approach, ' which communicates on more than one level.

Therefore, adults are more able to connect the dots of the cryptic sentences, which I use to describe some of the darkest points in my life. I also think it's essential to bring an element of humour to a speech in a natural fashion.

I'm not a theatrical and over-rehearsed speaker because I like the rawness of emotion within my speeches. One of the speeches I am most proud of is the one that I gave at my mother's funeral.

I have developed an emotional resilience as a speaker. I have spoken about my 5 Key ROI Marketing Principles, market research, getting social on social media, collaboration, confidence, Picasso, and snippets of my life journey, for example. I now feel compelled to talk about my emotional health to help others.

Every written speech enables me to decide what aspects of my life to cover, and my delivery provides control of my emotions as I speak. That one person drives me, the one who resonates with me and that needs to hear what I have to say.

Speaking has changed my life. One person is all the motivation I need to deliver talks that inspire, educate and entertain. When I looked into the audience of those 160 people, I looked for their response which suggested that my one person was there. A nod of agreement, a furrowed brow that means someone is listening intently, a deep breath of realisation taken in or the break of concentration when someone realises the hidden truth. I am there too, analysing evaluating my speech. I can hear my words fly as my thoughts process. There is no longer a rabbit in the headlights, just me standing in my power looking for that one person.

CHAPTER 2

Loving Myself to Freedom

By Angela Roth

The autumn sun is shining through the beautiful stained-glass window at the front of our Church; the dust motes are dancing in the sunlight, the colours reflected onto the walls; I watch, fascinated. The vicar speaks, 'Now one of our youngest members will read for us.'

I climb down from the pew and walk to the front. I'm wearing my favourite red dress, the one Mum made for me, and I walk up the steps, turning to look at every one. I've never stood here before; it's pretty scary!

For a moment, I'm not sure what to do, so I smile, and one by one, as I look around, lots of people smile back; it makes me feel happy, but suddenly I notice Mum nodding at me, pointing to the paper I'm holding: I nearly forgot – I'm supposed to be reading from it!

You may wonder what purpose this story has? You see, this was the day I had my first taste of public speaking; I was five years old, and I enjoyed every minute of it. I loved the quiet as everyone waited for me to start; I loved seeing the pleasure my reading gave to them, but what I most treasured was listening to the comments I heard people say to my Mum after the service ended. You see, although I was smiling at everyone, so many of them thought that my smile was just for them, and it had warmed and touched them; it made me feel like I'd given them something precious. This memory has had a profound effect on my life, though I was so young, and because of it, there has grown within me a desire – or even a calling - that I am here to touch the world with God's love.

Therefore, you might think that I would have chosen to pursue subjects at school that provided opportunities for speaking or performing in public; that would have been a natural choice, wouldn't it?

Yet I didn't. Although I took part in everything I was asked to do during primary school, my transition into secondary school brought me a very different experience, one that robbed me of my self-confidence, one that robbed me of my voice.

Come with me to a very different scene - one in which another smile plays a profoundly significant part.

I'm standing in a room full of excited girls – about 30 of us. We're all wearing the pristine, black and white uniform of Birkenhead High School for Girls; the school, all the parents, want their daughters to attend; the school, my dad says, where futures are built, and I'm the first one from my family to achieve a place there, a scholarship place.

It's our first day, and I'm excited and very nervous; I don't know anyone else, and I'm worried I won't make any friends. I remember Mum's words to me this morning,

'Angela, you'll be fine; you never have any problem getting to know people.

There'll be other girls there, just as nervous as you, find someone else on their own and give them that lovely smile of yours. Before you know it, you'll be the best of friends!'

I look around, but no one seems to be on their own; they all seem to be talking to each other happily enough. Then, I see a group of three girls standing a little further back from me. A tall, dark-haired girl talking to a shorter, blonde girl, but the skinny girl in the middle isn't joining in; she looks a bit like one of my sisters, with curly red hair and freckles; I'll smile at her. I wait for the right moment; after what seems like ages, she turns and looks at me, our eyes meet.

I begin to smile, but even as I start to do so, the smile is frozen on my lips as I see the strange look in her eyes; it's not a kind look; I don't understand it; it feels like a look of hatred. I don't know what to do, I want to look away, to look somewhere else, anywhere else, but I can't; our eyes are locked together.

Suddenly, the classroom door opens, and the spell is broken; our new teacher walks in, calling us to settle down and find a seat. My heart is pounding, but I move silently towards the nearest desk and slowly begin to sit down; and then I feel it, a slight brush of someone behind me, and a whisper, a cold, cruel whisper, 'What are you doing here, Fatso? You needn't think you'll find any friends; I'll be making sure of that.'

Then it's gone, over in a flash, yet lasting through decades, and the girl has moved away to sit at another desk; I sit, and as I do so, my world crumbles.

Have you ever experienced something that's been over so quickly that you aren't even sure it happened in the first place? Something that changes everything, that turns life upside down. If you have, you'll understand that such an event can be fleeting yet still have the power to affect you profoundly. My secondary school life became very different from what I'd expected; the joy and excitement had gone, replaced by fear and insecurity.

It became an uphill struggle to make friends, even to feel like I deserved to have friends. The whispered taunts, the digs, the knocks, tripping me up as I walked past, all of this was my constant companion.

Something else changed in my life that day, something completely unplanned, something that changed my life as I had known it. I discovered a new friend; I found Chocolate. Walking home to avoid meeting the bullies at the bus stop, I found a little sweet shop I could pop into on the way; there began my love affair with Cadbury's Dairy Milk, a love affair that was set to last for several decades to come.

Along with Dairy Milk, I found another ally in one of my older sisters, Helèna. Four years older, she was always kind to me, and I enjoyed the games we played.

She listened to my problems at school; comforting me and making me feel loved – you see, I couldn't tell my parents; they were so proud that I'd got my place at the school, a school where dreams were made, and I didn't want to destroy that illusion.

Of course, I know now that they would have been into the school like a shot if only I'd confided in them, but the bullies had convinced me that no one, not even my parents, would believe me, so I kept quiet.

In Helèna, however, I found the listening ear I needed; I discovered that she too had been bullied, and for the same reason, for her size. Helèna knew how I felt, she could empathise, and it gave me the courage and strength to keep going. She showed me that I wasn't alone, and I think, now, that our shared stories gave her the comfort she needed too. We didn't just share stories, though; we also shared secret trips to the chip shop on the way home from Guides on a Friday evening. Did this help? Of course not, but we didn't understand that then; we just took comfort.

Over the following years, I encountered both good and bad times, as all of us do. I married my wonderful husband, Dirk, and we had four beautiful children together.

My weight continued to go up and down, depending on whether I was dieting or not, and for many years I took to calling it 'baby weight'; after all, I wasn't alone in that! But inside, I wasn't happy, and I hated myself for the times I ate secretly, hiding the wrappers deep down in the bin.

But, in 2003, a tragedy occurred that shook me to the core. My beloved sister, Helèna, could cope no longer, and she made the irrevocable decision to end her life.

She left no note; perhaps she'd hoped she would be found in time, but I knew the pain she'd carried all those years, and it was heart-breaking to realise she hadn't found an answer to it.

After the initial grief and trauma settled, I decided to deal with my weight problems once and for all; I couldn't bear the thought of finding myself in that place of despair, and I wanted something good to come out of the pain. I joined a local weight loss club, and in the space of 4 months, I lost four stones. I was elated – I believed I had conquered my battles and would now live at a healthy weight for the rest of my life.

I was so convinced that when our consultant retired, I trained for the job myself, believing that I was all set to stay at my lifelong dream weight and help others do the same.

I couldn't have been more wrong.

I struggled with my self-image, and the pull towards eating when dealing with stress was never far away. On the face of it, however. I was coping well until a seriously stressful situation arose within my own family. As I sought to support one of our beloved sons through a hugely emotional problem, I lost my self-control completely. My old eating habits came back with a vengeance, along with the weight. I was devastated; there I was, regularly standing in front of groups, supporting them on their weight loss journey, yet steadily gaining weight, hiding it as best I could with shapewear!

I felt like a total fraud, and I knew I couldn't carry on like this; something had to change. But what? I'd tried everything out there in the past, and I'd never found the answers.

I had a decision to make; either I give up on my long-term desire to live at a healthy weight, or I look inside myself to find the answers.

The first was a non-starter; I knew I could never be happy if I did that. The second sounded scary, yet also exciting – after all, who knew me better than I knew myself?

Who knew me well enough to understand why I kept returning to habits that were destroying the very thing I wanted most? And why was I calling these habits 'treats', or saying, 'I deserve this', about behaviour that only took me further from my dreams!

And so, began my journey of self-discovery; slowly, I looked back and discovered when and why my behaviours around food had changed. Gradually, I began to take control by releasing myself from the pain of the past and choosing not to let the past dictate my future anymore.

As I began to see results, my self-confidence started to grow, and my weight began to drop! I was so excited; I wasn't just feeling healthier, I was feeling emotionally stronger too; I discovered how to love myself to freedom, and I wasn't going to return to the guilt led diet-mentality I'd lived in for so long. I'd developed strategies that worked – and they didn't include keeping bowls of chopped carrots in the fridge to snack on when all I wanted was Chocolate! But funnily enough, I could now eat a piece of Chocolate and stop – no more having to eat the whole bar – or even the entire box!

I realised I couldn't keep this secret to myself; I knew I had a deep desire to pass on what I'd learnt, so I developed my programme – the Shape Shifters Blueprint™ – showing others how they too can love themselves to freedom from emotional eating!

Will I stop there? Not while the world continues to develop flawed ideas to tackle obesity, like sugar taxes and plain packaging on chocolate biscuits!

I will continue to speak out and find a way to make my voice heard – a voice for all those who live under the burden of unhealed emotional pain that has dragged them down the path of eating for comfort. I will speak out until they discover how to love themselves to freedom!

CHAPTER 3

The Journey

By Ellie LaCrosse

"Stop being a chatterbox!"

From an early age, I could "chatter". This was at odds with my quintessentially shy demeanour and a complete surprise to my parents. Although I was the older sister, I always pulled rank and shoved my sister forward for any new experiences and would keep quietly out of the limelight.

This has led to an unsettling feature that surprises many people who think they know me.

"You're NOT shy! You're always so bubbly and talkative!"

The Journey

The seeds as a natural presenter and public speaker were sown and scattered from graduating from University and my developing professional business careers during the late 1980's- to the early 2000s.

There has been a learning curve with my oratory skills, delivery, and storytelling like all apprenticeships.

My professional speaking skills were honed *after* University. After graduation, my first job was with a top advertising agency in Birmingham around the late 1980s. I'd blagged this much sought after role as an Account Executive after jumping through the hoops of selection.

Advertising in the pre-digital era was a glorious environment of high net worth individuals, big budgets, long business lunches, exotic film-shoot locations and enough booze at events to keep everyone mellow and being surrounded with talented creatives. A heady mix for a 23-year-old.

By the end of my first working week, I was feeling pretty smug with myself that I at least knew how to prepare very fancy coffee for the MD and knew the route to the stationery cupboard, guarded fiercely by the secretaries.

The following Friday afternoon, I had the summons to see the MD. He possessed a very plush office - glass windows streaming in with light, expensive cabinetry and leather chairs.

"Ahhh, Ellie- sit down, settling in, okay? Good, good! Right, so your Director has just had confirmation from our client that we have a 'go' on developing a new campaign. He's suggested you're just the right, bright young thing we need on our Presentation Team for our top account," He gushed.

"Well, it's their Drivers Club events they want handling….got to pitch for it next week, down in London at their HQ", he handed over a bulging folder.

"There's the background- take it home this weekend and get up to speed on the prelims and campaign aims; Derek (the Director) will fill you in", he rattled on, "Need fresh ideas, ideas, ideas, got it? Questions? Oh, by the way, I'll be getting the team together and filming you on our new video recorder…. I thought it would help polish up the presentation to watch it back. Love my gadgets….Great! Well, that's it for now. I'll have a fresh coffee thanks…off you trot!" he barked.

I staggered out of his office, somewhat dazed. I'd barely managed to find my way around the building and catch everyone's name, and now I was being asked to *talk to one of the biggest corporations!*

I passed my Director's open office door en-route to my desk, and he caught sight of me clutching the large folder.

"Helloooo! Ellie, isn't it? Coming up for air yet? Want to grab some coffee and swing by for a chat - I'll introduce you to the Shell team."

This was 5 pm on a Friday- my heart sank a little, any ideas of skipping out of work on time for a girlie catch up in the pub evaporated.

What the rest of the seasoned Presentation Team initially thought of this green-as-grass, rookie presenter, tacked-onto the main presentation was quickly revealed when it came to the practice run-through with the MD a few days later. The MD (at the time) had a huge state-of-the-art video recorder on his shoulder, filming our practices.

Initially, I wasn't too nervous delivering my set piece from an overhead projector whilst seated staring into the large lens of the video recorder.

It was only minutes later, at the 'de-brief' where we were all crowded around the table peering at the screen, that my initial humiliation hit me, as all my flaws and faults were going to be analysed and commented upon:

"Need to slow your delivery."
"Sounds like Minnie-Mouse!"
"Look…look at the tapping foot….it's distracting."

It was an absolute trial-by-video camera. I learnt a massive amount in that office, 'on-the-job-training' and about dealing with constructive criticism. Useful but a painful introduction to the adult world of work.

The following week, as I sat at the back of the MD's huge estate car with some of the team, my anxiety levels started to rise. We entered Central London, arriving at the venue hall of this top multinational company by the side of the Thames. The hall was cavernous!

There were far more people seated in the hall than I was prepared for, but I swallowed hard and remembered my Director's words at the practice, "Look above the audience's head, take deep breaths to steady your nerves, then, tell them *what* you're going to tell them, *tell* them, then, tell them *what* you told them."

For training purposes within the office, the MD filmed the entire pitch; when we returned to our office in Birmingham, hours later for the de-brief, my Director sidled up to me and whispered, "Well done kiddo, first effort and all that, I'm sure the client team appreciated your pitch but, to be honest, I bet they were distracted by your shapely ankles and your right foot constantly tapping the leg of the stool you were sitting on!... It's just nerves; you'll get better!" he smiled.

Years passed, more adventures, life changes and careers later - communicating, presenting topics, research and speaking have all been at the core of my competencies.

Eventually, I'd had enough of working for others and decided to set up my own company and be my own boss.

I always enjoyed networking events to "show & tell", and being the consummate "chatterbox" never really had an issue breaking the ice with new contacts.

I had developed a company, Maison Frais Ltd., focusing on renovating traditional family homes and future-proofing and adapting those homes to help with the real dangers of falls and hyperthermia. The greatest killer of the elderly is in their own homes.

I had the skills and contacts with trades to help and support my father when his mental health fell into sharp decline in his mid-eighties. I had tried to broach the subject of adapting the family home, making my parents final years comfortable and safe, to keep them out of institutionalised care. To adjust the home to have care live in, if necessary.

By 2017, my new company was making good progress and establishing my brand. However, just before Christmas 2017, I experienced a personal family tragedy that has affected me greatly and coloured and influenced my life choices since.

Suicide is still considered a taboo subject. The fact suicide touched my family is something that has put me on a speaking pathway from the heart to the present time.

I will never forget the phone call from my brother-in-law. We aren't particularly close, so it was unsettling when he asked immediately to speak to my husband. The reason was to break the news that my 85-year-old father had committed suicide by hanging himself in the family home.

To even begin to forgive my father for inflicting this terrible, violent act and the impact it's had on our family, I have to explain a little about my father's character. He felt like he was losing control of his life. He'd made it very clear over the years he wasn't going into care; he'd say, "Ship me off to 'Dignitas', don't want to be a dribbling old codger".

Of course, we always discounted what he said as 'Dad-speak'. When dad gave up his car, his various ailments got on top of him; he felt his vitality and purpose slipping away. He didn't wish to be a burden to us, and his mental health declined into a deep depression, to the extent he dispatched himself off as efficiently as he knew how being an ex-engineer; it was quick, and there was no coming back. It was final.

Dad was old-school; his generation of men would never talk about their mental health. We later found out as a family, at my father's Inquest, his GP had repeatedly asked my dad if he had felt suicidal and did he want CBT? (Cognitive Behaviour Therapy). He might as well of asked him did he want to go to the Moon?

When I reflect on how we didn't listen and respect my father's true wishes and how brave and alone he was in his final minutes on this earth - it still breaks me down.

I use this in my speeches and talks to groups connected with designing buildings and Over-60 Community groups to raise awareness of the issues surrounding the impact the family home has on mental health. I'm perfectly able to talk dispassionately about my dad's suicide and the family tragedy. I know I have empathy with some of the issues my audience can have, and if I can get my audience to start those tricky conversations with loved ones, I feel it's been a job well done to raise awareness.

My speaking journey is continuing, albeit with a shift in focus. I've recently relocated to Cumbria, to the Furness region (the South Western Lakes and Peninsula). The Covid-19 Pandemic had caused me to pause, take stock of my life and prioritise what gave joy and meaning to my life.

I feel this has been a common theme for many, a weird sort of life 're-set'. I'm currently excited to renovate our Grade 2 listed historic property. I plan to convert part of the house into a bijou, cosy Writer's Retreat, aimed at writers who need space to create and come away with a feasible plan to publish their words.

Our office is a part studio, and I continue to interview published authors and writers about their writing journey to become published on my podcast 'Little Red Typewriter'. Now with the imminent release of my first poetry book 'Shadow Time'- A compilation that celebrates all the flavours of life. I've developed a talk called: 'Revenge Is A Dish Best Served Korma.'

It's a wry and witty poem in free verse where I explore the devastation in relationships from betrayal.

It's based on an actual incident that happened to me whilst I was in Poland, during the late 1990s and in a relationship with a fellow Tutor at the language school I was teaching in at the time.

A female friend betrayed me. I later sought my own back by inviting them round one evening to my apartment in the centre of the Stare Maesto (Old Town-Warsaw) for a homemade Korma curry meal, as part of a wider group of mutual friends from the language school. We were all terribly 'grown up' about the situation that had occurred six months previously.

Unfortunately, my little act of retribution was to prepare a separated korma dish for the offending couple - their dish was made from a can of dog food.

The great joke was that this couple kept going on how tender and tasty the meat in the curry was. I sat quietly, smiling enigmatically at my small victory, to salve my dignity and self-worth.

I'm a great advocate of non-violent acts of revenge and karmic consequences - I talk to groups about how all emotion is about living life, learning life lessons, and understanding ourselves.

We, humans, love stories; it's how we learn to cope with life. I enjoy telling these stories and sharing innate female wisdom with others.

Just beware, though, if I invite you to dinner with a Korma curry on the menu!

CHAPTER 4

From Introvert to Public Speaker

By Ian Llewellyn-Nash

A wise man once said, "...death & life are in the power of the tongue" [Prov. 18:21].

In my life, I have been honoured to speak to others in a range of differing contexts: as a nurse, as a father, as a preacher, as a coach, as an educator. I have spoken to groups of five, twenty-five, one hundred and five, even five hundred, and often to a single person. Yet, I am an introvert and struggle to speak to someone I may have only just met.

So, confession time: I am an introvert. However, I do enjoy it. I love my personality, and I love my quietness, my peace. I love stepping back, reflecting and then participating. I love being all that.

Being a speaker, I also love adapting to a speaking occasion and being as animated as any extrovert and capturing the hearts and minds of a group as a speaker.

Any speaker requires, in some way, a repository of information, insight, or content from which to speak. If we did not have that, we would be speechless and of little value to anyone. I also believe that how we show up as a speaker flows from who we are as a person.

Those so honoured, perhaps privileged to stand in front of others with dynamic content that encourages, stirs hearts and minds, uplifts and provokes deepest emotions, do so from, in my opinion, deep reserves of who we are as humans.

As a speaker, I am very aware that how I use my tongue to speak will affect my head and heart. Granted, to speak is to do so with purpose, relevance and influence. Such value to the hearer comes from my journey. My speaker's history.

I was born prematurely.

It was a Tuesday morning at 03.00 am hrs. Perhaps that set the scene for my life as I still have a hankering for turning up early and getting irked when folk are late. I was born in Northern Ireland to a Welsh Mum and English Dad. He served in the RAF (Spitfires and clandestine ops), which is probably where I got my military service genes from and a thrill for adrenaline and danger - having wanted to enlist in the commandoes and SBS. I grew up on the streets of Belfast in the 1960s 70s.

Consequently, I am accustomed to loud bangs - having had a few near misses with exploding bombs. Many a day leaving work, one would exit onto a gunfight in the vicinity of the place where I worked. I had had friends knock on our windows for help from my mum when they had been knee-capped (that's the sort of mum she was!). I grew up with soldiers visiting our house whilst on patrol.

I attended Orange Day parades - once ending up on the wrong side of town and getting thrown through a window! As a youth, I easily subsumed into the 'youth wings' of paramilitary organisations and gangs. Such was life! When I told my mum I would join the full paramilitary organisation – well, being my mum, she grabbed a stick and beat the living daylights out of me! I'm glad she did, as I guess I would possibly be not around.

At school I was good! Not at study - that was always a struggle. Having spent my GCSE revision time in hospital, I didn't get many O levels. But I was good at one thing - no two things! Football and athletics. Playing for the school side and another Youth organisation, I collected a string of cup-winner medals. At athletics - not only was I strong - holding the school record for the shot-put, but I was fast, very fast, and I loved it. To be truthful, it made running away from an attempt to smash windows a lot easier! I was the 100m sprint champion at school and across four counties.

A significant formative influence in my life was my 'mum'. She was phenomenal! She was brilliant! I grew up watching her being kind, compassionate and generous.

She poured out her life to others, for example, caring for someone with Alzheimer's before it was as well-known as it is today. She would take single mums in when thrown out by their parents, especially if they had had a baby – that generally didn't go down well with Roman

Catholic parents! She worked two, sometimes, three jobs to pay her way and keep our heads above the breadline. She modelled kindness and acceptance for me - which was a challenge growing up in a society that was intolerant of difference.

My earliest significant memory of my mum was when we moved out of our large house (owned) into a 12th floor flat (rented). Of course, it didn't dawn on me then, but we had been thrown out of our house due to the marriage break-up. Hence, I was blissfully unaware of the heartache that my mum was going through.

She could have got bitter. She could have – but she didn't.

She always put my sister and me first and went without when there was a lack. We became very close. Talked together, shopped together (providentially missing a few bombs going off as we travelled around the city). We laughed, we cried. I once bought her a 'Mother's Day' gift in the shape of a wall plate. It had an inscription written upon it. I appreciate that for some, these words may not ring true – indeed they may be hollow: but they echo what my mum was for me:

"You only have one mother
Patient, kind and true
No other friend, in all the world
Will be as true to you" [Anon]

I left home after leaving school and joined the Royal Navy. Between you and me, it wasn't a great start! I missed the boat. Not a good start to joining the Royal Navy- wrong time, wrong ship!

Ah well! Things can only get better… like marching around a square piece of cement being shouted at by a guy who could not pronounce his words. All I could hear was, 'eft', followed by 'height' Eft, height, eft, height… made little sense to me, yet somehow the body of humans I found myself in seemed to respond and move forwards! Or, being stuck in a metal room, 6x8 with pipes here and there full of seawater which all had holes in them so not only was it cold, wet and dark - it was a case of stop the water flooding in or get wetter, colder.

Or the other metal room, all dark and full of mist or gas as it turned out to be, or the other metal box full of smoke making you sound like Darth Vader every time you spoke because of the breathing apparatus!

But the food was lovely!

I loved the Royal Navy - absolutely loved it - it was fun. It was full of friends who would fight for you; some got confused on that point and would fight you. It was about friendship and being responsible and crazy at the same time. While in the Royal Navy, I began to be a 'speaker'. In that context, I found myself speaking to others about faith in the military.

As a medic, I was trained to be self-reliant in caring for trauma casualties and to diagnose, treat and recover. We took x-rays, sutured torn skin together, put on plaster casts, we would carry out emergency resuscitation etc. and prescribed drugs.

Confession: I am not a chiropodist. However, I had to deal with verruca's and such, like on the feet of the sailors and Wrens. I had a preference as to whose foot I was holding!

So, there I was in my first foot clinic, and a sailor came walking in for attention to his ongoing painful verruca on the sole of his left foot. The thing is, I had never done this before! But I couldn't tell him that I hadn't done this before. That would be silly! I would not live that down!

So, the thinking process went like this:- a verruca is painful on the foot. The verruca needs removing. Pain requires an anaesthetic. Removal in this case (and time/era) requires diathermy! Simples!

So... get patient to lay on the bed, with his feet elevated - cleanse area of verruca and apply anaesthetic. Look around the clinic area and spot a bottle of spray anaesthetic and, well, spray! You would - wouldn't you!

Okay, the foot area will now be numb from topical spray – so apply diathermy to cauterise verruca. I touched the diathermy probe to his foot – this was followed immediately by a three-foot-high flame. The patient shouts out, 'Doc, is that meant to happen?!!!!

Yeah (I said, swallowing loudly and looking as calm as I could – "it's burning the verruca away"!). Yeah, I know - I lied! But he must have had his verruca healed because he never came back!

I left the Royal Navy and went to college to learn how to be a minister. Speaking to others seemed a necessary part of that. Between you and me, though, I probably spent three years focusing on what to talk about rather than how to speak it! How to say that which abides within. That's the artistry of the speaker. The craft. The use of words. The use of pauses, the use of pathos, of humour. Using words to inform, to illuminate, to provoke.

The following words changed everything:

"I'm *sorry, Ian, I am sorry to say that the blood results confirm the diagnosis.*"

At this point in my history as a speaker, I had spoken words to many audiences. Those audiences sat in churches, or they sat in lecture halls. Audiences were made up of nurses, leaders, students. Everything suddenly seemed so futile. So, banal. So useless. So much driven by appealing to the head.

The blood results changed everything. The proving of faith. The proving of friendships. The proving of the very things that I spoke to people about to inform, advise, and encourage. Much of those early years and early treatment was framed by a single question: 'why?'

In my speakers' journey (I realised that everything shapes that journey and how we show up as speakers), the moment of change came a few years after that moment. I found myself in acute kidney failure on dialysis, questioning everything and everyone. Then I saw her! She was a stranger. Another patient. A young lady. She wore a white T-shirt with a meme printed on the front:

'Feel the fear and do it anyway.'

In that moment, a shift took place that would (re) shape how I showed up as a speaker to the one, or the ten, or more. Words without heart are arguably mere sounds. I went on a journey to learn how to speak not simply to the head but the heart.

I dedicated myself to coaching and developing the person in the mirror. I embraced people and speaking skills such as emotional intelligence, neurolinguistics programming; I qualified as a coach, I trained to show up as a person and not just a voice. Anyone can utter words.

I spent years doing that very thing. A crisis of health, faith, and mortality reoriented my thinking and being from simply speaking words to living the words that I said. (I'm not perfect, I have downtimes).

My speakers' journey has taught me that speakers should recognise that words build up or tear down; our words add value or detract value.

Through our words, we are building the world. Speak wisely; speak with honour, with integrity, with transparency: and remember your speaking style may differ from another's way of speaking.

Lived Words count if you wish to build lives wisely.

CHAPTER 5

Encountering Obstacles

By Jamie Wallace

I have a unique Speaker's Journey. I am not like the rest of the authors in this book, and I am okay with that. I love that fact! I have trodden a different path to reach this point, and I'm going to use the following few pages to tell you all about my journey into psychology and delivering the various messages of my way to date.

As you read this, I would like you to imagine you are in the same room as me, listening to me present my Speaker Journey, standing right in front of you.

My name is Jamie Wallace. I am a Speaker, a Coach and a Psychologist.

Growing up, I always thought I was normal, and I was made to believe there were people worse off and better off than me. I think this is something we could all relate to at some point in our lives, isn't that so?

Psychology teaches us about perspectives and focus and how each of us sees the world through our own eyes. I have always related to this but only recently come to really comprehend and apply it in my life effectively.

Perhaps you have heard of Plato's cave analogy? Plato starts from a very inward perspective and opens up the mind to new opportunities as new layers are added from what is happening inside the cave and then outside the cave and then considers the difficulties of returning to the cave once the mind is aware of all these new perspectives. His allegory of the cave helped me and those I have been coaching to grasp the concept of the different perspectives we can encounter in life.

Have you noticed how your friends, family, and others have different views on things?

Maybe they see things differently or hear your words differently, or perhaps feel differently to you in certain situations? I really find this fascinating, and now I am aware of this; it has helped me understand people and react to them more positively.

You see, in my wee world, growing up in the old ecclesiastical village of Lesmahagow, there were the landowners and families who had either earnt or inherited their fortunes, and then there were the folk from 'up the top' in the wooden flats and council houses which were not so well off and reliant on state welfare. And then, in the middle, there was us. Not poor, and not rich!

Growing up as a teenager and young adult in the West of Scotland, I would observe and take in what was happening all around me, spotting life's inconsistencies and injustices. My speaking practice then was limited to home and primary school domains, where I would pen short plays and poetry and later perform them with a show or recital for family or classmates.

In my twenties, while doing a course in Scottish Literature at Glasgow University, I was introduced to the concept of duality. I realised that this had given Scots like me an excellent opportunity to understand life on the British Isles better than, say, someone in London or another English province who generally would only see things through a London or British lens (which is usually an English or London-centric lens). In Scotland, we get the news of England a lot and news of Scotland with a British bias thrust upon us by the media. I would imagine it is rare to get constant news updates from Scotland in England. During my time at college in Glasgow and at university in Potsdam, I would learn about propaganda, how the media and press operate, and ways to get noticed to share the messages I wanted - for reasons of leisure, business or politics.

The more I explored duality in my own life; I came to recognise that from a very early age through the British education system that was in place in Scotland while I grew up, I was brought into this colonial world of division and segregation.

Of Public v Private education. Of Catholic v Protestant, Christian versus Muslim. Rich v Poor. Homeowner v Tenant. British versus European. I was, however, fortunate to have experienced the emergence of the European Union. This institution brings together a group of countries to create and harness peace, fairness and social inclusion. This would be the backdrop from where I would navigate and grow up in my formative years that play a part in helping me shape the way for my speaker's journey.

Family, community, society and peace are all values I hold dear and have played a big part in what I would soon recognise as different cycles in my life. Understanding our values deeper is essential when bringing about our internal peace.

One cold dark rainy evening, about twenty years ago, there was a knock on the door. It was a gypsy traveller from a nearby town, Larkhall, asking to see if we had any household belongings or clothes for her family and community.

I could see the pain in her eyes and resolve that it was a task that had to be done. You see, a few days earlier, a gang of local bigots decided to set fire to their homes rendering their community homeless.

This mother, now destitute, had to rebuild her family's life. She received a bag of clothes from me. She also offered to read our palms for a small fee. My mum, older sister and myself all got our palms read. She was good. She seemed to know things about me that only I knew! But the one thing she said when talking about love and relationships was that I have three rings in my life. I always wondered what was meant by this - three relationships? Three marriage proposals? Something else? Today, I understand its significance as being more holistic and representative of my life's three cycles I have come to recognise.

My first cycle is representative of my secondary and higher education and my introduction to working life from the age of 12. I am not even sure this would be possible today for young people to develop a work ethic early, which is a pity. I see myself as quite fortunate.

During this time, I decided to settle down with my first proper boyfriend and got my first decent job with McDonald's and then a hospitality company. My time at high school, college, and the university would help me develop my social, language, and communication skills, provide me with travel opportunities, give public recitals of my writing and participate in school performances. All part of my speakers' journey.

I always saw myself as a bit of a philosopher during my formative years. I would reflect on my life and dig deep into my past for evidence of my being. Reflection was a skill I learned on my own. It helped control my mental health and gave me direction in life.

In 2000, I spent a few months intensely researching my own life of 20 years and dug out material evidence of my timeline to date. Amazingly, all of the things we forget are hidden away in the back of our minds.

I later realised that this same practical process I undertook is used in some cognitive behavioural therapy methods.

The psychiatrist Fiona Murdon also endorses the approach in 'Defining You'. In her book, she also praises the importance of reflection - after all, once we know and understand our story, we can then help move forward from the present.

I would value people and relationships over most things, and I felt strongly about trust. You see, one day at high school, my best friend broke our trust, and as a result, I hid away from friendships until I started college in Glasgow.

Speaking and coaching involve a lot of trust - and I have been able to bounce back from my experience of losing my sense of trust, which puts me in a strong place when building rapport and relationships with those I meet.

Today, I am skilled, trained, and certified in timeline Coaching, meaning I can take clients through a similar reflective journey in a few hours instead of a few months.

The difference between having someone walk you through the process and doing it yourself is a no-brainer.

From the practitioner point of view, it brings me great joy to see those aha moments when the light bulbs go off as connections are drawn during the conversations.

I see my second cycle as having taken place between 22 and 32. During this time, I was in my first salaried job, completed a Business School Degree in change management, set up a business and a community group, ended things with my boyfriend and went out with my 2nd boyfriend. I gained a reputation for putting Scottish sweets on the Internet in my confectionery business.

This allowed me to give talks in Glasgow and London at business networking and student enterprise events on my startup journey and e-commerce. During this time, I would also go back to Glasgow University to do a degree in the Gaelic language. During a year of study at Sabhal Mor Ostaig, I would get involved with a new Celtic Students conference. This would bring me Gaelic speaking opportunities at conferences in Cornwall, Wales and Ireland, where I would discuss my research and expertise in the Social Media of minority languages.

In my third and current cycle, which started around 32, I achieved my Gaelic honours degree and embarked on a postgraduate Masters in Psychology with the Open University. I set up and folded a business to support my research in the Gaelic language and recently set up a coaching practice to complement my work in psychology. I would work for the London 2012 Olympic Games' organising committee and Glasgow's 2014 Commonwealth Games. I would double up their Gaelic spokesperson and participate in a Gaelic documentary about the Games. At the time of Scotland's 2014 Referendum, I was a speaker at organised events in Wales and Skye. I would share a platform with prominent politicians and community leaders like Leanne Wood and Ian Blackford.

This cycle brought about a slow burnout and realising that my life would need to change drastically.

As such, I took up new travel and long-distance walking opportunities and got involved in Psychology and coaching.

I now talk about the transformation I went through since walking the Camino de Santiago and the challenges I currently battle to get back with my 3rd boyfriend, who lives halfway around the world, cut off by travel restrictions for two years since the global pandemic struck.

During the Covid-19 pandemic lockdowns, I spent time getting to know myself, and through understanding my timeline, I have realised that each development cycle of my life has been rooted in relationships, education, and work issues and that each process lasted about ten years. This has been a game-changer for me. I have come to realise that what defines me is not the circumstances I was born into but my values and beliefs, which, if I choose, I can be fully in control of.

Following the recent challenges and opportunities brought about by Covid-19, a new chapter in my speaking journey is now beginning.

A journey where I am less discerned, and one that is more focused and directed by love - after all, as I have come to learn over the past few years since completing the Camino de Santiago, #LoveIsTheWay. And this all leads up to where I am today...42-beyond Psychology postgraduate degree, marriage, home, travel... I am looking forward to future speaking opportunities at conferences, meeting rooms, private gatherings, and media as a new cycle in life opens up for me.

CHAPTER 6

A wonderful place of gratitude

By Jeanne Zierhoffer

As a strategic results-driven coach, corporate trainer and International Award-Winning Speaker, and "The Implementation Queen", I chose to make a difference in other people's lives. I'm grateful for where I am today based on the decisions I made in the past. All of my choices have led me to exactly where I am today, which is in a wonderful place of gratitude.

That wasn't always the case; as a young child, I had extreme difficulties communicating with other people, feeling like I was consistently putting my foot in my mouth and was socially awkward. With no tools at my disposal, I chose drugs and alcohol to become the life and soul of the party, or so I thought.

In the late 1980's I chose to conquer my battle with drugs and alcohol, which wasn't easy. For six months, I became an in-patient within a halfway house in Dorchester, MA. It was a battle, but I knew it was well worth it,

After getting sober, I started my first job, and the young ladies I worked with were a little abusive, bullies, to be more precise. Being a little emotional, I took everything personally, as if they went out of their way to make my life miserable.

That's when I started my personal growth journey. It had nothing to do with me and everything to do with them. I completely shifted how I spoke to them and when they noticed they didn't bother me anymore, they stopped.

Today, I am an empowered leader, a leader of leaders! As I wandered through my journey in life, I became a life-long learner, absorbing personal and professional growth.

I have fallen many times, which doesn't matter.

The only thing that matters is how I STOOD UP again, and what was the lesson? I continued on my journey of personal and professional growth to understand that it is an inside job. The more comfortable I am with myself, the more significant my impact on my community. I surround myself with like-minded people and have a network of professionals I call my friends. I have two coaches and three mentors, and I don't reinvent the wheel. I put my spin on it based on my past and present experiences making it unique.

I often received the comment "it's easy for you," Is it? Or do I choose to go for my goals and my dreams?

I believe that we all have a choice, we all come to a fork in the road, and we choose to go left or right. The decision is ours to make. I have made many bad decisions in my life; I have taken the wrong fork in the road on many occasions. Today, I choose where I go and what I do, based on two questions;

1. Is it going to take me closer to my vision?
2. Is it aligned with my mission?

When the answer is yes to both of those questions, I say yes! If the answer is No, I state it's not aligned with where I am headed in my life today.

Do you know the pain points of your target market or the topic you speak on? Be the solution to the pain point in your talk; know your industry. For example, I am the meat & potatoes consultant in my consulting business. Why? I saw a need for simplicity in the structure; many business consultants overcomplicate it and over-whelm their clients.

Here is a sample of what that is;

"I teach the simplicity of structure, keeping it simple like meat and potatoes. I add no fillers or by-products, yet it will be a fantastic dish, just like your journey with me. This may sound bland; I will make sure that it is rich with content and purpose, just like sinking your teeth into a wonderfully prepared filet, with no bones to spit out.

I am a leader of leaders. I work with people who value simplicity and structure, and we are a team. Meat and potato consulting cooks with the highest level of ingredients and care. We put people first, show up as servant leaders, and eat our cooking. As the hostess, too, you are learning how to build relationships and rapport, starting with "Hello". Getting clients faster results and the freedom to add individual spices to their meat and potatoes.

I excel in my purpose-driven mission of 'Each one, Reach one, Teach one, with a safe place for them to learn and grow within the community. We add more dishes and processes as we grow together, creating soufflés and adding side dishes that complement our meat and potatoes. As you take the steps with me, we start to expand, adding our dessert menu; think of it as the icing on the cake. Take ownership of your business, just like a chef in his kitchen, and let's cook up a fabulous menu together."

Do you see, feel, taste, smell, and understand the message in keeping it simple, like meat & potatoes, then layering on as we move forward? When people can connect to your speech in a way that they are starving (in this case) at the end for what you have or you give them the solution, it's a win, win.

It was back in 2015 when I thought about speaking in public. The thought of being on a stage in front of thousands of people was terrifying. No way would I ever do that or wanted to do that! Then it crossed my mind, and I realized I had a message; I realized that we all have a message to share, and when one person hears our message, whatever message that is, we create a ripple effect and could help many people! That didn't come easy; I was the woman that sat in the back row and did NOT raise her hand. On the day I did raise my hand, I had a quick little question, which turned into a HUGE shift in who I am today. I raised my hand quickly and put it down. The man on stage in the front of the room with 500 people saw my hand go up and down. He pointed.

"You in the back of the room, I saw your hand go up and down. Would you please stand up?"

I waved my hand and shook my head and said no, I'm good, I'm all set, thank you. One of the crew ran over to me with a microphone. When he came to me, I said no, I'm good, thank you, I'm all set. The gentleman from the stage again repeated,

"Ma'am, stand on up and grab that microphone. What's your question?"

At this point, I didn't even remember my question anymore. I didn't want to stand up, and I didn't want to be seen, I didn't want to hold a microphone, I'm the woman in the back of the room in the last row, ugh!

Once again, he asked me to stand up, "grab the microphone and tell me your name,"
I held the microphone down by my belly and told him my name.
"I can't hear you; please hold the microphone up at your mouth,"
He began mimicking the action of holding the microphone up.
"Tell me your name."
Jeanne Zierhoffer, I said very quietly.
"I didn't hear you, speak louder into the microphone,"

This back and forth continued for another few times until I spoke into that microphone and felt the walls shaking, with my name bellowing out of it. My hands were sweating, I could feel perspiration rising, and all I wanted to do was just run to the bathroom; I just wanted to run out of the room!

He started to ask me a series of questions, and the microphone kept dropping downwards. I would whisper the answers, and he would repeat the exact words...

"Hold the microphone up to your mouth."
He proceeded to ask me a few different questions.

We never got to the question that I had, a good thing as I completely lost the question. This process I went through went on for about 5 to 10 minutes, which entirely changed the direction of my life.

Walking through one of my biggest fears of being seen and heard, holding up a microphone and bellowing my voice through that entire function room. I lived through that. It was nothing, it was simple, and it was easier than I had imagined. I am forever grateful.

The fear was still there, but I knew that it wasn't going to kill me. Kelly Clarkson sings, "What doesn't kill me makes me stronger", and that was an entire speech that

I did in New Delhi, India. Look at your past and look where you can get the most beautiful, unique speaking topics based on your individual experience. I sit at the front of the room, raise my hand, jump on stage, and speak in front of rooms with 100's and 1000's of participants.

There are so many things that I could write to you about regarding how to be a speaker but ask yourself these questions;

- What does that mean for you to be a speaker?
- What does it look like for you?
- What does it sound like for you?
- How are you seeing yourself on stage?

Working with so many trainers and training companies, my learning accelerated. I learned how to anchor and time myself on stage.

I wanted to make a more significant impact on my audience, so I asked myself these questions:

1. How does my audience see me?
2. How do they hear me?
3. Do they feel me?

I talk about personality values and how to talk about your system, structure and expertise you bring to the table. Listen and look for those clues with the people who want to build relationships and rapport with you, the people who want you to get to the bottom line and tell you how much money you're going to make! Which of the above resonates with you? That's most likely who you are connecting with within your audience.

I want you to connect with all of the above, understand that we all hear and see differently, learn who you are and how you are showing up first, then learn how to craft your talk to everyone in your audience.

CHAPTER 7

My Social Enterprise Journey

By John Reed

Until 2016 I had never heard of or even been aware of the type of business I now own, a Community Interest Company commonly referred to as a CIC. However, that year fate took a hand, as it has on many occasions in my life, when I met Mr Andrew Mullaney, who worked for Lloyds Bank as a Business Connector.

We met in a Networking Group organised by a local Accountancy practice, and he encouraged me to consider forming a CIC. In time this advice led me to do just that, but my public speaking journey began immediately when I decided to win a specialist course that would train me in how to do this properly.

To enable me to join the training group delivered by The School for Social Enterprise in Birmingham, I had to speak to a group of 10 people who would decide if my idea was what they were going to fund. And so, my "pitch" was necessary because, without the training, I would not have the knowledge and the funding available to me to begin trading.

I was, of course, very nervous, and decided that to stand out from the crowd (there were many more people applying than could be accepted), I would have to be innovative, to ensure that I was seen as worthy of their trust, and to demonstrate that I would benefit from the course.

My presentation was to last ten to fifteen minutes, and I needed to describe what the project, if successful, would be, how it would improve the situation of my intended clients, and how sustainable it would be long term.

The innovative idea I had was to present the main part of the speech as a news item.

I was to begin by turning away from my audience and pretend to be a radio newsreader, announcing that "John Reed has today formed a new company here in the Midlands, which will benefit many people". I then turned to face my audience to give the details they had requested.

This way of starting a speech was entirely born of my imagination, I had no idea how it would be received, so I was even more nervous about the outcome. When I turned around, I was faced with an audience who were smiling, and as I delivered the speech, I could see them accepting the concept as fulfilling all of their criteria. Therefore, it proved that innovation in speech-making was an excellent way to deliver something different, and that lesson has stayed with me throughout my journey.

In truth, my journey into Public Speaking had begun years before. In 1969 I applied for and won a place on a training course that my employer, The North Thames Gas Board (a nationalised corporation), offered to my sector of their employees.

They needed skilled workers to teach the younger generation of apprentices the skills of the trade. Time had given me a special skill, relevant only then and for a few years later, so I was chosen for a place.

This was a promotion, I became a salaried member of staff, which allowed me to develop my speaking and teaching skills in a controlled environment. I enjoyed the work and experienced a genuine love of speaking.

Occasionally the audience (the students) were hostile because not everyone enjoys learning. Looking back after all these years, I can see that this was a valuable experience; it taught me to be myself, speak clearly and concisely, and not be afraid for the audience to see "my vulnerability".

Two years later, I got married. After the ceremony, we had the Reception and, of course, the customary speeches.

My best man, Tony Ballard, opened the proceedings in a very "usual" way.

He complimented the bride on her choice of groom, and then it was my turn to reply.

In retrospect, what I said on the day was probably not well written or delivered properly. I tried to follow the time-honoured way of shaping and delivering the speech. Indeed, it was well-received, but criticism is not expected in this scenario.

But my journey continued throughout my career. The key to my "success" is always speaking as "me". Nowadays, this is called WYSIWYG (what you see is what you get), but all of my life, I have only acted in an honest and up-front way, and to this day, all of my public speaking serves to demonstrate who I am. In effect, I "sell me" to my audience, and in return, they allow me into their lives. The result is that my speeches are honest to the core, high value, and worthwhile.

Fast forward 47 years, goodness, is it that long. During this period, 1969 – 2016, I established many types of business. Some were very successful, some less so, and one failed altogether. But there is a common thread running throughout the time.

Nobody can start a business without having a plan.

That plan must be "sold" to investors and clients alike, so it is difficult to achieve that unless one is accomplished as a public speaker.

Often the audience is small, and regularly it is large, but whatever the size of the intended audience, it is crucial to plan the speech, rehearse it, and deliver it professionally. My journey has allowed me to develop my style; some would say "radical style", but I would say it is personal to me, and that is why I am so comfortable nowadays taking on any public speaking role that presents itself to me.

Let me expand on this theme because anyone reading this piece will understand that seldom do those who are successful in their chosen field share how they became successful. Ask any successful salesman the method they used to become so good, and rarely will you get a truthful answer. Why so? If they are earning high returns on their skill set, they generally will not want to see a competitor enter their field. Essentially, they are insecure and want to guard their income.

Compare that to my way of working, for I will share all of my life skills and experience with anyone who engages with me on a meaningful level. And why would I do that? Simply that I believe collaboration is a powerful tool; we can all learn from each other and together benefit. Now relate this to my career as a public speaker.

Twenty years ago, I had a successful business in the Security Sector. My products sold into large conglomerates such as Securicor PLC, to name but one. As a small enterprise, I needed to be heard and believed before these companies would engage with me and eventually spend considerable money with my company.

To understand their needs, I attended an exhibition, seminar or meeting that would allow them to get to know me better. This process also allowed me to learn what they needed in their business. Eventually, I spoke publicly at an event attended by a few senior Directors from the company and struck up a friendship with one of them.

Please note this was well before Social Media gave us all the ability to comment directly as it does today.

This stage of my career was nerve-racking, but I overcame my nerves by only speaking factually about a topic I knew a lot about and speaking from my heart directly to those who would slowly come to believe and trust in me.

And so, to the present day, let us return to the concept of "innovation". The reader may ask a straightforward question, "how can I innovate my delivery if the art of public speaking is so well documented and practised by so many successful people "? Again, I return to my basic theories, and that is that firstly you must understand the topic thoroughly you will be speaking about, and secondly, you must somehow allow your personality to shine through and present to the audience a performance based on something different to them, but very familiar to you.

We are not all performers, but if you believe in your message and deliver it in a heartfelt way, the result will be informative and stimulating. The aim is to engage at all levels, react to any signals the audience may send, applaud, for example, and deliver in a professional way as possible.

I have always followed my heart, I have researched my topic and my audience, know the subject matter, have a clear objective in my mind, and then "go for it".

To do this, no matter what the size of the audience may be, you will need to be super confident, and this should come from following my tips above. Remember, you cannot over-rehearse this delivery, and once you have mastered it for the first time, then that speech can be repeated to as many different audiences as you can muster. And every time you repeat it, you will gain stature, confidence and professionalism. The speech will mature, and so will you. In addition to this fact, your skill will become more widely known, and more business will ensue, either to your sales of products and services or to your requests for more public speaking events.

Let's look at my day as it unfolds, the day I am about to speak to an audience of any number 10 – 1,000 – or more.

My day begins the night before, with an appropriate bedtime.

I need eight hours of sleep, so I decide when I will rise in the morning so that I know when to switch off the light the night before. After waking up, showering etc. and dressing, the next is the most essential part of the day; I enjoy my breakfast! I leave home in plenty of time to arrive at the venue a good two hours before it begins so that I can assimilate myself into the atmosphere of the event. I sit down, perhaps have a coffee, and ensure that all of the preparation I have done is now complete, and I can present with confidence.

Each event is different, but I must be calm and collected when I am called upon to speak. I check the electronics (my radio mike), and I walk out onto the stage as the organisers require. I wouldn't say I like anything on the stage other than myself, as this averts the eyes of the audience members from me, and that is not what I want.

I need their exclusive attention. I want them to hear every word, absorb every moment, and leave the event with some good memories of what I said at the end of the day.

In conclusion, I would say that my public speaking journey has been long, but that I learned it "the hard way" by making mistakes early on, by taking advantage of opportunities as they occurred, and by practising.

There is no easy route because if you aim to excel at this skill, you need confidence, you need to believe in yourself, and you need others to see the merit of engaging with you for mutual advantage.

I would add that this art, which I now consider is a thing I am successful at, is the most rewarding, and I would not have missed this journey for anything. I hope you, the reader, enjoy my writing here and look forward to meeting you one day in the future, where I can demonstrate my skill.

CHAPTER 8

Making an Impact

By Jose Ucar

Great speeches are powerful. They inspire people to be better, take action, think differently and change their lives in various ways. They stay in a listener's mind, much like an epic novel or a fantastic painting. And they move everyone who hears them in some way or another.

They may be swept along in a tide of passion, brought to tears by an emotional tale, or erupt in laughter because the speaker tells excellent jokes. Whatever the effect, the one thing that all great speeches have in common is impact.

And that, in essence, is why I speak. I want to have an impact on the lives of my listeners. I want them to take action that improves their fortunes. And I want them to call me when they want a professional speaker at their next event.

Early Experiences

I decided to take up public speaking when I was 12 years old. My favourite teacher, Marcos Subero, told me it was fundamental to success in life, and I loved the idea of doing it. Over the next four years, I gave plenty of presentations at school and started learning my craft.

When I was 16, I qualified for an exchange student programme called AFS after ranking 17 out of over 400 students. It was an exciting chance to go to Sweden and represent my country. So, I travelled from the warm Caribbean waters of Venezuela to the snowy northern hemisphere. It could hardly have been any more different!

Sadly, after all the build-up, I completely froze when I went on stage to give my first speech. I could not say a word, my mind went blank, I got sweaty palms, and afterwards, I had to decide whether to stay on the trip or give up and go home.

How was I going to represent my country if I couldn't speak?

I chose to stay because I loved everything else about the experience. I relished exploring an unfamiliar country and learning a new language. I also realised I could learn from my failure. So that is precisely what I did. I asked my favourite teacher at my school in Sweden to help me, I practised my speeches in front of 10-year-olds who spoke better English than me, and I soon gained enough confidence to go back on the big stage.

Becoming A Better Speaker

The choices we make at certain moments tend to define us. We find ourselves at a crossroads with one path that will take our lives in a particular direction and another that propels us somewhere else entirely – often with no opportunity to go back and choose the other route instead.

Looking back on it now, I am certain that the decision I made in Sweden was critically important to the life I now live.

I could have allowed my fear to overwhelm me and prevent me from following my passion for public speaking.

But I did not want to give up, and even at that age, I knew what I wanted. I learned how much I enjoyed speaking and performing in front of people. I felt a calling to communicate in different languages and share my stories and experiences with the world. I also knew that if I did not pursue my dream, I would have no idea what to do with my time back in Venezuela. I wanted to succeed and travel the world, and these ambitions drove me to carry on and get over the setback.

That transformative experience feeds into my coaching. I often say to clients: you can let the trauma put you off and stop you from taking risks, or you can learn from it and use it to motivate you. However, you react, it will have a ripple effect on other areas of your life. If you are afraid to speak in public, you may feel less confident about human interactions. Consequently, you will be less inclined to speak up in social situations, speak out when you have something to say, and share your opinion on a one-to-one basis.

On the other hand, if you deal with what's stopping you, you can improve your life dramatically.

You might think that I cannot be afraid when I go on stage anymore because I have done it so many times. Nothing could be further from the truth. I still feel nervous, and I still experience fear. The difference now is I know how to deal with it. I understand I am afraid because I care about what I do, and I am excited about it. So, I speak to my fear and say, 'Look, I've done this many times, so you're not getting in my way. You've just reminded me that I love what I do because it makes me feel alive.' In this way, my dialogue with myself helps me find a more resourceful state.

This resourceful state is vital when dealing with unexpected situations. If I go blank, I just smile and tell the audience I lost track of what I was saying, so let me return to it. And if I get stumped by a question, I just say, 'Great question. I don't have the answer to that yet, but let's connect right after this and talk.' Whatever the difficulty, I never excuse myself or try to hide my discomfort because that would affect the connection I am establishing with the audience.

Connecting with The Audience

My life is where it is today because I stand up and share what I know. I tap into my passions to tell stories, build rapport with my audiences and make sure they remember me. My presentations often lead to other opportunities, which I typically say yes to. I only think about the possibility of being judged or messing up for a few seconds before I dismiss it because I know it is much more essential to take the chances I get.

When I am on stage, I keep in mind that it does not matter how good my slides and audio-visual elements are if my audience is disengaged. So, I pick up cues to gauge how they are receiving me. I notice whether they chuckle, lean forward to listen closely or make more eye contact. And I see if they pull out their phones because that shows they are disconnected, which is the last thing I want.

There is no better way to engage an audience than telling a story. I often look at how comedians take their audience on a specific journey to make sure they are laughing the whole way through.

That is how they keep people engaged, and it requires meticulous planning to get it exactly right.

Although my goal is not making people laugh, I operate similarly. I carefully prepare every aspect of my presentation to ensure that what I say has maximum impact. This also helps a lot when it comes to managing nerves because I am much more confident about what I present.

However, even though I carefully plan my presentations, I am happy to improvise if the audience will respond better to something spontaneous. In this way, speaking to me is like a dance of mutual responsiveness – people react to what I say, and I adapt what I do based on their reactions.

Public Speaking Opens Doors

After I came back from Sweden, I completed a bachelor's degree in International Business and then went to Spain to do a diploma. This involved work experience for AFM Advanced Manufacturing Technologies, the Spanish Association of Manufacturers of Machine Tools and gave me the chance to visit Turkey, Brazil and Argentina.

It also led me to the event where I met one of the most significant individuals in my career: Alan Pearce. He invited me to come to the UK and work for his company SGS Precision Tools Europe Ltd, a cutting tools manufacturer that mostly made Aerospace tools. During my first spell there, I worked my way from packing boxes to Iberia Area Manager.

After two and a half years with SGS, I decided to take a full-time job at AFM. This enabled me to travel the world and represent the member companies in countries such as the USA, Mexico, Turkey, Brazil and India. I could tell my presentations were well-received because potential clients always came up to me afterwards and told me they wanted to speak to the business I was representing.

My public speaking confidence was growing all the time, and I was developing my skills and becoming better at my craft every time I went on stage. I carried this confidence into the next chapter of my career, which occurred back at SGS after accepting an offer to become their EU Marketing & Business Development Manager.

I presented and marketed the business in the USA, Mexico, and throughout Europe in this senior role. I built up some of their distribution networks and conducted interviews and open house events at their facilities. And I was proud to secure SGS a deal with one of the biggest aerospace manufacturers in the world.

Going Out on My Own

I thoroughly enjoyed working for SGS, and I still have an excellent relationship with Alan Pearce – we work so well together that he is now one of my clients. But I had known from an early age that I wanted to establish my own business one day. So, when some of the SGS clients enquired about training sessions with me, I finally made the jump and struck out on my own.

Since I started my own business and even during the pandemic, I have done at least a couple of presentations per week. I am on clubhouse every day for 90 minutes, and I also do podcasts, coaching sessions, speaking invitations and interviews. It is a lot of work, and I love it.

One of the things I relish most about it is knowing I can impact people's lives anywhere in the world through the power of the internet and social media. This inspires me to keep going when I am tired or do not feel like doing it. Because I know I am making a difference in people's lives, I stretch myself and grow when I push myself.

I also love that people now seek me out because of my reputation. If they did not know I existed, I would not help them. But I can because they know who I am. This is one of the reasons I enjoy marketing. I know how important it is, and I teach clients how to raise their profile and stand out to connect with people, deliver their greatness and serve them in a way that helps them achieve what they want.

If I ever need extra motivation, I just remember my childhood. I was not given many things while I was growing up because my parents and grandparents could not afford them, which motivated me to earn them for myself in the future.

At one stage, this led me to focus too much on money, and other parts of my life suffered as a result. But eventually, I found a healthy balance, and now I am more focused on helping others grow as I grow with them.

That's how I live my life and how I want to live it going forward.

With this in mind, I think it's vital to be authentic. A business partner recently asked me to speak about building a six-figure business. But I knew I had not done that yet, so I did not feel I could talk about it. I know about plenty of things – like speaking with an accent, struggling with a new culture, or starting from scratch and building something. So, I am happy to talk about those things because I know I can share something valuable with people. And the more I learn and experience, the more stories I can tell.

Even though I have accomplished a lot, I am not finished and I am never going to be. My work is always going to evolve. There is no end to my career as a speaker because there will always be people out there, and there will always be things to talk about. And the more I know and learn and grow, the more impact I will have.

CHAPTER 9

Mission to Help Others

By Mildred D. Muhammad

Becoming an award-winning global keynote speaker was the farthest career in my mind. It wasn't on my radar at all. However, it is the most rewarding career I could ask for. I'm proud of the speaker I've become as I continue to study my craft to become better.

I was a victim who became a survivor, and now I'm a warrior on the issues of domestic abuse and violence. I never thought I would be a victim of domestic abuse either.

My life has taken so many turns that I never thought I would be living. I've learned many lessons, and I use those lessons to help others avoid the pitfalls I suffered so that their lives can be better.

The Beginning

My story began in late 1999 when I asked my former husband for a divorce because of the abuse I was suffering. That did not go well. Shortly after, he moved out and began the long cycle of emotional, psychological, and financial abuse and harassment.

As the judge read my petition for a restraining order, he said, you need to get away from this guy. I said, 'Your Honor, I'm trying to do that". He gave me a lifetime restraining order because of the threat he made to my life. He said, "*you have become my enemy, and as my enemy, I will kill you*, but visitation was included in the order until a custody hearing was scheduled."

My former husband told me that I would not raise our children alone. He decided to keep our children and leave the country during an arranged weekend visitation. It would be 18 months before I saw them again.

Since a custody hearing had not taken place, the law says he has the same right to take them anywhere he wants, as I did. They call it *'custodial interference'*. That's still breaking the law, but no actions were taken to resolve the issue by law enforcement. Although I didn't know where they were, others close to me did know and didn't tell me. However, they would report back to my soon-to-be ex-husband regarding my movements. They took his side and believed the lie he told them, which was that I had asked him to take our children away because I didn't want to raise them.

To make a very long story short, in September 2002, a gunman and a young boy were killing innocent people in the DC Metro area. That gunman was my former husband, whom you know to be John Allen Muhammad, the DC Sniper. Law enforcement told me that I was the target. They put my family and me into protective custody until he was caught. The theory was he was killing innocent people to cover up my murder so that he would come in as the grieving father to gain custody of our children and receive $100k compensation given to the sniper victims.

The media did not report the hardship my children and I suffered during that time. I was running and hiding from him for two years. Once captured, the community began blaming me for the crime. The public was totally in the dark about my side of the story. They said, *"if I had stayed with him, he would have only killed me. If I had stayed on the West Coast, then the people on the East Coast would be alive. How dare I call my children and me victims when none of us were hurt or killed. And how dare I bring this drama into their quiet community.* They weren't supportive of my family and me.

I began self-isolation because going out to the store or anywhere became a nightmare. Others recognized me, and they were not kind with their comments. I would dodge people, wear disguises, and turn around so no one would see me. However, I had to muster up the courage to go out to try to find work to take care of my children.

The few jobs I had were not paying enough to sustain my family. I prayed and asked God to give me a position to make enough money to have our place, provide for my children and be home when they needed me.

My First Speaking Engagement
A domestic violence advocate, Norma Harley, contacted me to share my story for the county's upcoming event on

domestic violence. I presented her with every reason why that would NOT be a good idea. When others blamed me for my former husbands' crimes, how could I do that? I thought they would throw eggs at me, or worst-case scenario, someone would kill me when leaving an event. She stood 4'11" and stated not to worry; she would protect me! My thoughts were all based on fear, so I decided to attend even though it was an unpaid event. After sharing my story, I received a standing ovation. Public speaking wasn't as bad as I thought.

Next Steps

After that event, I decided to pursue this speaking career. Before going further, I had to talk with my children about it. I called a family meeting. I told them that I needed to help other women victims of domestic violence by sharing our story about their dad. I told them I was asking their permission. They looked at me with their beautiful precious eyes and said, 'Mom, you do what you have to do and always tell the truth about their dad'. They gave me their blessings.

I began to study the craft thoroughly. I went to the library checked out a book on becoming a public speaker.

I contacted the author because there is a sample contract and questionnaire available in his book. I did not want to infringe upon his copyright or be sued for using his information without his consent. He asked why I wanted to use his knowledge. I explained my situation, and he said, you have my permission to use the contract and questionnaire in my book. So, I tweaked it to my topic, and I was ready. I googled 'domestic violence conference', and several came up. I picked one, sent out an email and within 5 seconds, I received a response asking for a quote. I didn't think that far. So, I gave them a price to include accommodations. They agreed, and instantly, I became a paid Professional Keynote Speaker.

I began looking at different ways to obtain speaking engagements. I signed up with several speaker bureaus and continuously looked for engagements on my own. Since I did it the first time, indeed, I was able to do it again. I was successful in my pursuit.

I decided to expand my reach to the military community because John was in the military, and (*post-traumatic stress*) PTS became a topic. I expanded my knowledge regarding post-traumatic stress, and with that came the learning that military personnel are not the only ones that suffer from PTS. Victims of domestic abuse and violence and others living in hostile environments can be victims of PTS as well.

I explain the perils of PTS (*post-traumatic stress*) that soldiers suffer when returning from a war zone, as well as victims who are diagnosed with PTS. I am recognized, and I've received awards throughout the military communities for the championship of the Family Advocacy Program and their mission to educate, promote and end Domestic Violence in Military Communities.

My Accomplishments

Today, I'm an Award-Winning Global Keynote Speaker, International Expert Speaker for the US Dept of State, Certified Consultant with the US Dept of Justice/Office for Victims of Crime, CNN Contributor, BNC Contributor, Domestic Abuse Survivor, Certified Domestic Violence Advocate, Advisory Board Member & Instructor for The National Resource Center on Domestic Violence Speaker's Bureau, Sexual Assault Advocacy Network's

Advisor, Best-Selling Author, Former Internet TV Talk Show Host, Trainer & Educator as well as a Certified Professional/Personal Development Consultant.

I travel and speak on a global platform to discuss my life of terror, abuse, and heartache while promoting Domestic Abuse/Violence Awareness and Prevention.

Published Author

My first critically acclaimed memoir, Scared Silent: When the One You Love Becomes the One You Fear, was published by Simon & Schuster in 2009. I self-published two working journals, "A Survivor's Journal" & "Dare to Heal", as well as "Planning My Escape" *(a comprehensive step-by-step safety plan)* specifically for victims and survivors to help with the emotions that others may not understand and to leave an abusive relationship strategically. My second and last memoir, "I'm Still Standing: Crawling Out of the Darkness into the Light", has been released. My new eBook addressing domestic abuse/violence during COVID-19 is titled "Being Abused While Teleworking During Coronavirus Disease 2019 (COVID-19) Pandemic: A Safety Guide for Victims of Domestic Abuse/Violence & Awareness for

Bystanders" is available on Amazon. I have co-authored three books: The Mom in Me, Media Circus and Ari'el Rising.

-

Awards

I have received many awards such as a 'Special Commendation presented by the Office on Violence Against Women', 'A Proclamation presented by Prince George's County Council for her exemplary role in the fight against domestic abuse/violence, Maya Angelou "Still I Rise" Award, 'Shirley Chisholm Woman of Courage Award' and 'REDBOOK's Strength & Spirit HEROES Award', 'The Telly Award', 'ACHI Magazine Woman of Inspiration and TV Personality of the Year', as well as multiple awards from the military community, non-profit organizations, and other agencies... to name a few.

Documentaries

I have appeared in the following TV shows: Lifetime Movie Network Series, "Monster in My Family"; CNN documentary, "The Minds of the Sniper"; TruTV documentary "The DC Sniper's Wife" produced by award-winning producer, Barbara Kopple; Discovery

Channel, "Who The Bleep Did I Marry"; Investigation Channel Series, "Escaped ~ The Sniper's Wife: Episode 2; MSNBC documentary, 'I Married The Beltway Sniper": syndicated TV show, Crime Watch Daily and Vice TV, "I, Sniper".

Interviews

Mildred Muhammad has been interviewed on Dr Oz, Oprah: Where Are They Now, Anderson, Ricki Lake, Katic Couric, Issues with Jane Velez Mitchell, The Mike Huckabee Show, TruTV In Session, Larry King Live, The Tyra Banks Show, and Good Morning America, and has appeared on BET and other local and national TV interviews. She has also been interviewed by various national and international radio shows, internet radio, national and international newspapers, and internet blogs and magazines worldwide, including the BBC, NPR, Essence, Jet, The Washington Post, and Newsweek. She has also been recognized as "One of the Nation's most powerful advocates for victims and survivors of domestic violence". WROC-TV, Rochester, NY.

Conclusion

As the ex-wife of the DC Sniper, John A. Muhammad, I continue to share the very personal details of my experiences involving fear, abuse and, many times, victim-blaming. This experience has allowed my mission to be even more influential with greater purpose.

I share my expertise on what it's like to be a victim and a survivor of domestic violence *"without physical scars"* to various conferences, seminars, workshop audiences which include victims and survivors of domestic violence, advocates, law enforcement professionals, therapists, counsellors, mental and medical health providers, university, and college students as well as to conduct military personnel training regarding domestic violence.

My authenticity is as remarkable as this unforgettable story of abuse.

CHAPTER 10

Permission to Dream

By Nikie Piper

For many years I've had the same vision, the same visualisations, the same image, the same deep inner paralysing fear inside. Every guided mediation or journey I have ever travelled resulted in the same singular vision, no matter the format, venue, music, or guide. A sizeable empty stage with me standing on it, an audience as far as I could see, lights low, way, way out into the distance, casting silhouettes of the thousands upon thousands of people standing in the darkness, packed tightly together, the energy expectant, hopeful. Thousands of grey people are standing still and quiet.

My microphone stand stood in front of me holding a single large-headed microphone, and what little backlighting there was shining up from below the stage somewhere behind me, highlighting the heavy, dark curtains that hung floor to ceiling of that vast space. The image seemed black and white the first time it came to me; on subsequent visits, I feel perhaps it wasn't, rather just the absence of light.

Many years before those visions, my first public speaking experience was completely unplanned and unprepared for. I was attending a work event of around 800 people to whom my manager was due to give a technical presentation on a research & development project we were working on. Twenty minutes before he was scheduled to speak, he was taken ill. All eyes turned to me, at the time a project coordinator and with absolutely no idea of what was on his presentation or of the in-depth cutting-edge technology the project was researching: I was there to collect contacts and business cards.

My heart flipped then sank at a million miles an hour, closely followed by an equal velocity of fear (read sheer panic) rising through my stomach, my chest and pounding its way into my brain. Oh no, I can't, not me, I don't know anything about it! My mind is fighting furiously for a way out. At that moment, I knew there was no one else, and it was inevitable that I would be stepping on to that stage in less than 10 minutes. I don't remember much about those last few minutes before I stepped from behind the blue velvet curtain onto the stage and up to the lectern. I do remember the sea of expectant faces, the heat from the spot lamps, the giant screen (where do I stand so that I'm not in the way?), the laptop showing something different to the screen and my mind telling me a million other things.

To this day, I have no idea what that presentation was about. With my heart in my mouth, I projected my typically softly spoken voice and spoke what I hoped was clearly and loud enough. I introduced myself, apologised on behalf of my manager and launched into the first slide – self-preservation taking over. It was over before I knew it.

I did give that presentation; I know I pretty much read word for word from the slides, for a few seconds as I started to speak, my mind somehow telling me I couldn't just read them out, then acknowledging that I didn't know anything about that project so I would have to, the microphone sounded hollow, the room quiet and my voice nothing like my own.

The audience clapped and sang my praises for my last minute volunteering and asked far too many questions about the presentation and the work that I couldn't answer. I am eternally grateful to the event host for fielding them away. It could have been the stuff that nightmares are made of, but looking back, I am genuinely grateful for the experience. It taught me a lot: that I could, the experience wasn't that bad, that I had a voice. Yes, it wasn't as I'd have wished to do it, but I did it, and if I'm honest, practically no warning was probably a good thing, or I may not have ever done it!

From that point, I thought I would have developed a real fear of public speaking, well, more than I believed to be normal at any rate, and I did to a certain extent.

After all, isn't that one of the highest-rated, most common fears ever? Isn't it amazing what we choose to believe? I used to watch in wonder at speakers that had a great affinity with their audience, that seemed so happy and go-lucky, almost unscripted if you like; it seemed like a foreign art!

My journey through life has taken many turns since then, but I have found that the more passionate I am about my subject, the easier speaking about it is. I'm not sure where my passion for sharing my work overtook the fear of speaking to an audience, but it did somewhere along the way.

These days I step into my passion and share my messages from my heart. I'm learning to embrace what I'm passionate about and share as the real me; after all, my speech isn't for me. It's about my audience and what's in it for them. What I can share with them to help them, make their day that little bit better, or what I can teach them.

Fear creates barriers that seem so real.

My lessons from my first speaking venture taught me it's OK to be new at this, with not being perfect, with gaining experience, you have to be willing to make a mess of it and still do it anyway because what you have inside of you will light the way. It will guide you: what you have inside you is a gift to many.

I learned to be kind to myself, and I realised ways to tame your brain when the fear kicks in. When you understand that some fear reaction is inevitable, you can manage it more. Through conversations with various people that speak, I began to realise that being nervous is just normal, and everyone feels something beforehand; it's not wrong, and it means you're human, and I'd be worried if there wasn't. One of the keys to speaking, as I mentioned earlier, is your passion: it guides your way once the adrenaline has subsided.

For me, the way I accepted that fear (it doesn't ever go completely) was to visualise that feeling as I thought it was.
Sometimes that was a wall to be climbed, sometimes avoided, and then I remembered that I get to choose how I want to feel, I get to choose my beliefs about how I show up, how I am on stage, and off for that matter, and my reality started to shift. Fear and excitement are the same chemicals in the brain; after all, the situation determines how we perceive it. So, I choose excitement.

It is said that the 'inner' work is the work for anything. A brilliant exercise for this is to Quantum Leap into your new reality. It works on you now and in the future and can help bridge the two paths. If you believe and genuinely desire to be a speaker or even step up your speaking engagements, part of your journey to 'there' is to step into your future self, to quantum leap into who you are being, feel it, visualise it, be it: live, breath and focus on it.

Journal around what it means to you, why you wish to do it, who is the 'you' you want to be? What's in it for your audience?

Journal around the different aspects, from the 'you' you wish to be and how that is different from the 'you' now, from the viewpoint of a participant in the audience on the receiving end – their experience, feelings, changes and impact you've made on them.

Look at every aspect from the gigs, process, people, venues, journeys, and results for all.

Tap into the feelings, especially those you have now and those you wish to have; what thoughts do you have and what do you want? Use it to determine how much and what preparation you need to do, lean into your perfect audience and what works for them, your speaking framework and what works for you, your authentic message and the real you. How are you being, and do you allow yourself to be you?

Use the power of journaling and visualisation to create, get clear, and change your beliefs and how you feel.

So, coming back to my vision, has it happened? Am I working towards it? The answer is I've no idea. But what I do know is that I don't feel fear around it now.

I used my pen to create the meaning I wanted for it, and it now sits in my subconscious, waiting. I am ready for whenever that moment arises, and I'm looking forward to it.

I'm relatively new to the speaking arena, where I share my passion as I write this. But as I'm stepping into more and more speaking roles, my inner work and journaling are paying dividends. I love sharing my message and taking this powerful tool out into the world.

Like many, I looked for help, and there is a lot of excellent support out there, whether that's free or otherwise.

My advice would be to work on you first, get clear on the points I made above, take the time because that is what you will ultimately fall back on.

Your heart knows; your mind can create it, and the action you take follows.

Journaling should be every professional's, entrepreneur's, business owners, network marketers, coaches, leaders or consultants go-to tool to help them get from stuck to unstuck, to change their direction, to change their mood, to raise their vibration, to start to create the life that they truly love and truly want, and to let go of everything that isn't serving them.

It becomes more reflective and creative when your brain is free to create and feel, free from the must-dos and the 'I don't have time' thoughts. Trust me; it's a left-brain/right-brain relationship.

The other great thing about journaling is that there are no boundaries, no rules and plans, no filtering, no overthinking, and no self-judgement, just letting your heart flow and seeing where it takes you.

If you can imagine the magic, you can *create your magic*. All it takes is thought and action. Your mind is the most powerful tool you have, and if you start believing more in the power of journaling, who knows where you'll end up!

So, if you're not getting the most out of your journaling practice – or your speaking career - or indeed if you want to start one then, as an Empowerment Coach, I invite you to reach out or join my Facebook group – @The Art and Soul of Journaling - and learn how. Let me show you how I created a journaling practice that has turned into my real life.

Journaling – it's not just writing; it's creating the magic for your life.

Dream, vision, journal, then create. Create more of what makes your heart sing, your eyes sparkle and your soul soar and watch your life change. Make your motto be, 'All in, no matter what.'

All things are born of dreams, so give yourself permission to dream and bring those dreams into your reality.

CHAPTER 11

A Journey of Beliefs

By Philip Horrod

Have you ever wondered how you became the person you are today? Or why your life turned out different to the one you had planned? If not, you must be one of 'those lucky ones' who carved out your life exactly how you designed it.

Strangely, I've yet to meet one of these 'lucky people'. If you are one of these people, please get in touch with me. I'd love to know how you've managed it.

The rest of us are more likely to have arrived at where we are today through a mix of our decisions, how well we have dealt with life's routine ups and downs and how we've handled the unexpected events life can suddenly throw at us now and then.

Those life-changing events which spring up out of nowhere when we least expect them.

Losing my Mum at the age of 12 was one of those events. Losing my family home twice were two others. So was utterly burning myself out during my corporate career at the tender age of 50.

None of these events had figured in any part of the plans I had made for my life. However, each of them played a massive role in shaping my future.

When I began to reflect on these seemingly random events, I realised there was a hidden connection between them. It was a connection formed from my own beliefs. Beliefs I didn't even realise I had at the time.

This realisation sparked my interest in writing and speaking publicly about the connection between our life events and our beliefs. Each of us has hidden beliefs, which have developed in response to our own unique life experiences. Beliefs that influence our lives, which we usually don't even notice.

However, when we gain awareness and understand these event/belief connections, we allow ourselves to manage our lives differently. We empower ourselves to take control, rather than our hidden beliefs being in the driving seat for the rest of our life journey.

Ultimately, this helps us achieve something everyone wants; to live a happier and more fulfilled life.

Looking back, the event/belief connections I noticed in my own life developed way back when I was a child.

My childhood was the best of times until I reached 12. It was the worst of times after.

The turning point was when my Mum died from a form of cancer. She had kept it at bay for several years through sheer willpower and determination. Right up until the day my Dad came home, he told us he'd had an affair, they had a child, and he now needed to leave us to go and take care of his new family.

My Mum went into hospital and never returned home, passing away a short time later. Overnight, my Dad went from being my childhood hero to the Devil himself.

As a result, I turned myself inwards, internalising my thoughts and feelings to the point where I needed counselling and a bunch of pills to keep going.

I will always be eternally grateful to our Grandparents for agreeing to bring up my brother and me from then on. I'm not sure where either of us would be right now had it not been for them.

Most of my teenage years were a blur to me, like trying to drive in dense fog, unsure of which way to turn to escape it. That fog got even thicker when my Dad went bankrupt as I turned 18.

Just like my Mum's death, I blamed my Dad for his bankruptcy as well as for all the upset it caused, like losing our family home. He had gone to sea aged 15 and spent his career on cargo ships, working his way up to be a Captain.

So what had made him think he could successfully dabble in the business world, which he knew absolutely nothing about?

Fast-forward and the second family home I lost was during my divorce when I was 35. We'd known each other from our school days but drifted apart when we realised we were heading in different directions and found ourselves simply wanting different things.

During our marriage, I'd completely thrown myself into my career and studies to qualify as a management accountant. I succeeded in both but paid a high price as a consequence.

After remarrying, I spent most of my 40's working hard and long hours again, this time to enable us to buy our own home and start the family we both wanted. Somewhere along the way, though, I lost sight of why I was working so hard in the first place. I ended up working 14hr days, through weekends and during our holidays, mistakenly thinking I was doing all this purely for our family.

Eventually, my mind and body reacted by 'exploding' one morning while I rushed around to get to work yet again. My arms suddenly felt like lead. My heart started pounding like it was trying to burst out of my chest. As I slumped into a chair, thinking I had a heart attack, my wife called 999. Thankfully the paramedics arrived quickly and whisked me off to the hospital.

Once there, what we thought was a heart attack got diagnosed as a severe panic attack, brought on by the intense and ongoing stress I had been under.

Although I had narrowly missed having a heart attack, with hindsight, I sometimes wish I'd have had one. It may just have been easier to handle than what subsequently happened:

After getting the all-clear on the heart attack front, I got referred to a mental health unit by our GP due to the impact my stress had taken on me.

It was like my head had exploded and sent me back into the fog I had experienced as a teenager.

Except for this time, it was denser than ever. So dense that I lost all insight into pretty much every facet of my life.

Things were so bad I was told I needed to be sectioned. Things went from bad to worse after the police had to be called when I decided to go missing. Not only had I lost all insight, but I had also become paranoid, thinking the whole world was against me and trying to lock me away.

At first, after coming out of the hospital, I had rebounded, overjoyed that I hadn't died from an actual heart attack. Little did I know this was just the start of a severe manic episode, where my thoughts and emotions began to soar as high as a kite.

Another symptom of mania is that of uncontrolled spending. In my case, I ripped through our life savings, justifying my behaviour in my mind as being entirely rational. With hindsight, it couldn't have been more irrational.

For some inexplicable reason, I decided it was a good idea to buy two new cars, a van and two motorbikes, all at the same time. Never a dull moment when you're experiencing full-on mania!

Months went by, and the fog eventually began to lift. At least enough for me to be allowed to return home again.

However, my manic period was quickly followed by me falling into the depths of depression. It was like being in an aeroplane, nosediving towards the ground after suffering engine failure.

I honestly have no words to describe the sheer never-ending black hole that is depression. I can only say I was utterly desperate not to exist anymore, firm in my misguided belief that everyone I knew would be better off without me.

I felt that same desperation every day for about six months. I regularly made plans to turn my misguided belief into reality but thankfully managed to cling to life by my fingertips.

I gradually made it through one day at a time, thanks to my faith, family and friends. Without these, I know I would no longer be here.

While I was off work, my employer had kept in touch and offered me a different job to return to. Very kind of them, but I could no longer return to work. It was all I could do to get up in the mornings, let alone get back to chasing sales targets every day. Finally, I was let go on medical grounds.

It felt like I had gone from being somebody to being a complete nobody. No confidence, no job and no more sense of purpose. I felt less than a nobody due to the stigma which still unfairly surrounds those who suffer from any mental health problem.

I hid away from friends to avoid being asked how I was doing. I sat in the dark to avoid being seen. I binged on TV to avoid having to think about anything whatsoever.

We decided it was best for me to become a stay-at-home Dad. Not the career I had ever planned, but it did help make up a little for all the time I'd lost not seeing our children grow up while I had been chasing all those ultimately unimportant material goals.

Becoming a stay-at-home Dad also gave me time to question where everything had gone wrong and what had led me to make all my mistakes. I talked this through with a fantastic therapist and coach, who gradually guided me through my recovery process. She helped me accept, challenge and change, which finally enabled me to move on and plan for the future. A much better future.

This reflective time made me realise how my need for career success and a higher salary had come from feeling like I had lost everything when I was younger. How my desire for financial security had come from the insecurity I had felt. How my belief that no one could ever truly be relied on to be there for me had come from having felt abandoned by my Dad. Of course, all these beliefs were completely wrong in reality;

Apart from my Mum, I had never actually lost anything that truly mattered. I had never really been abandoned or lost my family security. My Dad had continued to support my brother and me through everything we ever did, both financially and by always being there whenever we needed him. Our Grandparents had also given us a loving and secure home, as well as all their kindness and wisdom.

My belief that my Dad had purposely ruined our lives could not have been more wrong either; His affair was born out of his own need for emotional comfort when he knew his wife was dying. He just happened to meet someone who coincidentally needed similar comforting at the same time, after her marriage had ended.

His bankruptcy had come about from his honourable best intentions of paying those who relied on him when he didn't get paid himself.

My belief that my Dad wasn't there for me also couldn't have been further from the truth;

When I burned myself out, he was immediately at our doorstep, helping and supporting my family and me. He had never not been there for me.

It was me who had avoided him, rather than the other way around.

While massively painful at the time, my burnout turned out to be a hugely beneficial wake-up call for me. It got me away from everything I was doing wrong in life. It got me away from working every hour of every day and away from all my misguided beliefs. The very beliefs that had caused the breakup of my first marriage had caused my burnout and been the cause of so much heartache for me and all those around me.

My new awareness of all this gave me a renewed sense of purpose. I retrained as a coach in my desire to help others avoid and recover from their burnouts. To help organisations support their employees to avoid the potential pitfalls of work-related stress that I had fallen headlong into.

I was lucky enough to gain the time, space and coaching I needed to identify, challenge and change my beliefs that led me to burnout in the first place. Now I can help others identify and change their own beliefs, so they can avoid all the pain and heartache I went through.

I also now speak publicly, as I want as many people as possible to know that challenging and changing misguided beliefs helps prevent the effects of burnout. It helps in a way that sleeping well, eating well and taking long walks in nature can never do.

Of course, self-care is both sensible and essential, but it can only help someone manage their stress symptoms better. It can't fix the true, underlying root cause of their stress or remove the real causes of burnout.

While undoubtedly beneficial, more sleep, broccoli and dog walks won't save you from burnout. Challenging and changing any misguided beliefs you have will do.

CHAPTER 12

The 3A's Approach to Happiness

By Ritu Sharma

Awareness*Acceptance*Action

These three words can sum up my life journey so far.

So, I can give you some background; I was born to well-resourced, socially well-placed parents who were culturally conservative but also educated. I was the second daughter and was not welcomed in their world.

The cultural setup did not go in my favour. Although a large family around me surrounded me, I grew up lonely and quite un-noticed.

Now, as a fully-grown adult, I can look back and see that my family truly believed that their restricted and pruned upbringing was for my good and that I was a difficult child as I questioned everything.

So, with this understanding, all was done that could have been done to crush my spirit, affecting my self-worth and self-belief directly in a negative manner.

I was academically average until I got to do what I wanted to do, studying Language and Literature for a master's degree, and I excelled. I was 21 years old then. I went on to being a teacher and continued to do so for the next 20 years, and I thoroughly enjoyed that.

I loved sharing what I knew with my students openly, not just about the academic curriculum but also about life, beliefs, and personal development.

What I didn't stop and see was that my approach to life, over the years, had become that of a survivor, not a thriver.

Inherently, my dial was permanently turned into survival mode. I had been lost as a young girl and a young adult.

I had attracted a toxic partner because of being an empath and had gone further into a pit of shame and guilt over the years. Social setups had not made it easy for me either.

I was only brought to my sense of urgency to change my mindset while I was at rock bottom consciously; there was no further going down. What could be done? Why was I going through this? What can I do differently to make life better for me?

All these years, I had felt like an outcast, someone who was exclusive to facing gender-based discrimination, manipulation, cultural pressures, suicidal tendencies, financial abuse, DV, homelessness and God knows what! Only to realise later in life that I was no different to thousands of other women facing similar experiences and challenges on a day-to-day basis.

Then why was I so oblivious that all these practices of control oppression were common and that of the distraught existence of many women? The answer is simple: I was unaware.

I did not know that gender was systematically being used as a tool to keep women subjugated. I have had enough personal experiences to understand how these techniques lower one's self-confidence and self-esteem and rip one's soul apart.

The questions that came to my mind were:
If this is such a common problem, why aren't enough people talking about it?
Why do families allow this to happen?
Why aren't these women coming to the forefront?
Why are we still silent?

And then it dawned on me that we are still worried about being judged. We still feel ashamed to accept that we have been treated in a derogatory manner, and we have allowed this to happen to us. And that victim-blaming is more common than we'd like to accept.

I was character assassinated by my ex-husband when I decided to walk away from my marriage. I decided to call it quits. It was my decision. Probably the best I had made in my entire life by then. I was devastated back then to know that he was talking ill of me.

This was done to silence me.

I was frustrated, angry and hurt. Not just for myself, but all the women who were going through coercive control, modern slavery, DV, abuse, cultural pressure, or anything designed to break our spirit. I was hurt!

On the way, I learnt some valuable lessons that made my vision clearer:

The world owes you nothing
Change is the only constant
You are your Creator

This was my phase of acceptance. I accepted everything about me and my life: the good, the bad and the ugly. After this acceptance, I never felt the need to fight anything or explain myself to anyone when misquoted or misunderstood.

I was ready to break my silence and stand up for all who were either silenced or ignored. At the same time, I understood that the meaning and reason of my life was to serve.

I qualified myself as a Coach and started my journey with this understanding. I had been a teacher all my working years, and I had loved my teaching job. But now, I had found something that fired my soul up. There was no way that I wasn't going to answer the call.

And so, I decided to change the narrative. I decided to accept the existence of manipulation, abuse and control in families, workplaces, and cultural setups. I decided to make a statement that families aren't always your support network. Not all parents are supportive; not all siblings share a great bond, families can be more toxic than strangers. That DV is as common as tomato ketchup in households and that women must speak up!

I decided to become aware, accept all that was and take action. I chose to speak!

I came across a quote from Carl Jung, 'The reason for evil in the world is that people cannot tell their stories.'

By not telling our stories, we empower the wrongdoer; we normalise being abused, we make it OK to be controlled. I did not want to add to the power of evil.

I decided to log my whole journey in my book 'Rich Man's ~~Poor~~ Rich daughter.'

The first time I stood up in front of a large audience, I spoke about times when I was seriously suicidal. Attempting suicide at 21 and then getting back to square one at the age of 36, when I was going through a divorce and being gaslighted, but I wasn't aware. I narrated the whole thing, emphasising the need to develop self-love and embrace yourself for who you are.

I felt vulnerable sharing my authentic story, struggles, and downside with a room full of strangers, but the need to voice my concern was bigger than any of my fears.

I realised that many in the audience connected instantly and later when they watched the video on social media. The video went viral.
This was just the confirmation from the Universe that I needed to strengthen my voice. I was so grateful to God. Still am. Always will be.

Since this speaking moment in 2018, I have not looked back. Since then, I have delivered hundreds of speeches, workshops, and online events and connected with some great like-minded individuals on their journeys. We are out to change the world.

I blatantly share my struggles with people, not for them to pity me but for two very different reasons:
One - Abuse for women is still prevalent, even now!
Two - It is possible to create a happier life, no matter what you have experienced.

I also bring into my speeches/talks/workshops elements of empowerment and emotional intelligence, Mindfulness, positive communication, and Leadership.

All these elements are something I truly believe each of us should tap into and help ourselves grow into better individuals. We all have a personal responsibility to create our best version in this lifetime.

I have acted on my advice and have spent the past few years in rigorous self-development programmes, leading to self-discovery and spiritual progression. I am thrilled at where I am right now, but I can feel that there is a lot more to come in my bones. I have accepted that this life is a gift from my Creator, who has assigned me some significant and serious work and that I must do my best to meet His expectations.

Although my quest is around empowering women, it is not anti-men. We need to learn to un-condition the conditioning we all have gone through and systems we have been following for centuries. Men are equally hostage to these as much as women are.

Currently, I lead a women's organisation, Kaushalya UK, that I found and head as a CEO. I am also an entrepreneur who is hungry to learn and grow, open to possibilities. I am a professional speaker and trainer who people seek to have onboard, especially women's empowering events. I am known as the 'Women Empowerment Ambassador', and I love it!

I look back at the little girl I once was hurt and neglected, who had no voice… I embrace that little girl and often tell her that she is loved, that she is enough, that she can change the world by changing herself first!

I say to the young lady who was gifted and talented but was labelled as a 'problem child' because she was inquisitive. The young lady whose spirit was crushed by social and cultural setups and injustices. I tell her that she is beautiful and that the world is her oyster. She can expand as much as the Universe, and she has all she needs to be happy in this life.

I also speak to the middle-aged, lost, and distraught Me and tell her to forgive! She did well by being resilient, stubborn, and surviving all odds. She can now relax. She can be at ease. She has done well by forgiving everyone who hurt her and caused her pain. Eventually, they all did her a favour by pushing her to a life of purpose.

This is one story out of millions.

What is your story?
Who are you?
Is this who you want to be?
Have you ever thought about what would the 'best you look like?
What are you going to do to create the best version of yourself?

Most importantly, when?

All you'll ever have to do to create happiness is, apply the **3A rule** and be Aware, Accept and Act!

CHAPTER 13

Born to WIN, conditioned to FAIL!

By Sam Dossa

From a very young age, I felt angry. Very angry.

I am not so sure about the reason. But the anger was there, and I didn't know how to react to it or manage it. I was about 5/6 years old.

My teachers would tell my mum, 'He is a good boy, a bright student. But his behaviour is out of line'. She was not happy when she noticed that I had learnt some foul language and started swearing and throwing stones at passers-by outside my house. I was furious.

I am the middle child. We are five brothers, and I am the 3rd one, right in the middle. I was born and brought up in Karachi, Pakistan, in the 1970s, in a close-knit community.

I had many reasons to feel safe and secure with a large family around me, parents, siblings, relatives, and a loving grandmother. I was blessed but still angry.

I was always very fond of my father. He was the towering personality in the house. Very smart and articulate, yet a real gentleman. He was an entrepreneur, ahead of his times, materialising his creative ideas. He was a community man dedicated to serving voluntarily, ready to help and offer his services. He was a great communicator, connecting with people from all religions and cultural backgrounds. He led us by example. He taught us to look at humans as humans without judging them on their social/cultural/religious labels.

I had the utmost respect for my parents but still failed to please them with any change in my behaviour. This unacceptable behaviour went on display for a long time.

I would get in fights, swear, throw things at others, even hurt people on purpose and feel no guilt or remorse. I was OK with my anger.

I did all this without giving it much thought. I just felt the emotion too strongly and did not stop to try and find out why was this happening or how could I possibly change this. I was just angry.

At the age of 7, I started following in my father's footsteps in community service. I joined boy Scouts Cubs and started offering help to serve communities. This gave me a good vent for my inexplicable anger issues. I began to calm down. This exposure also gave me a sense of belonging and a feeling of self-worth. I got into the habit of meditating and praying regularly. This was when I started to develop my leadership qualities and was active in sports.

I was pleased with myself. Finally, so were my parents. When I was 14 years old, the model of this world revealed itself to me. I started to understand that people only wanted to know you or valued you if you were of use to them. My family was going through times of financial strain, so much so that I was asked to give up school and look for work, which I did.

I started holding a stall in the market to sell perfumes. This was my first entrepreneurial experience and exposure to the working world. I enjoyed the experience and was grateful too to be able to get hold of some key entrepreneurship lessons at a young age.

During the same time, I went through a bad experience too. Amazingly, I felt guilty and ashamed for no fault of mine. Even more amazing that I have not spoken about this in all these years.

While at the market, I was sexually molested by a grown adult. I was lured and taken to a quiet place where this man tried to make sexual advances. I pushed him away and ran; I ran with all the strength I could find in my shaky legs. I got back to my market stand and continued as if nothing had happened. As I shook, I could feel the anger brewing back up. I decided to drown myself in work to block my anger this time. I never spoke about this to anyone.

I continued living, went back to education the next year and established myself as a successful entrepreneur in my early 20s. I also secured a leadership position in a reputed international company.

I migrated to the UK in 1996 for the next part of my journey, which culminated in a messy, manipulative marriage, leading to divorce and further trauma. I struggled to fit in. It was a different world altogether. I struggled to find work, maybe I was over-qualified for the jobs, or perhaps my accent. It took me a while to find my feet, but eventually, I did.

In 2004, I lost my mother to chronic depression and suicide while I awaited the arrival of my twin daughters. I was lost after this episode.

She was due to visit me in the UK from Pakistan soon.

I was devastated. One minute I was expecting to see her and the next, she's gone!

The most immense pain was that she had taken her own life. Neither my family nor I had picked any signs of her being in chronic depression. It was ironic that we have two health professionals in our family. Both are very well experienced and frontline workers. Maybe the close people are easy to miss.

I couldn't visit to pay my last respects at her funeral because of my responsibility with the mother of my children and my firstborn, who was only four at the time. This hurt me further, and I slipped into depression.

There were so many questions that I wanted to ask my mum. Why did she do this? Did I pressure her to come to the UK? Maybe she resented this. Was she unhappy where she was? Was something bothering her too much? How come my brothers and their wives had not noticed anything about her? I was so angry about the whole situation, and the more I tried to reason with the whats and whys, the further my thoughts got entangled, causing me pain and upset. I felt helpless.

Being a man started to feel like a curse. I was expected to have it all under control, and I didn't feel that way.

Social and mental pressure was building up. And I gave in. I questioned everything when I failed to see any hope around me.

I had built resilience since I was 14. I was fed up!

I started getting counselling, which relieved me and helped me manage my thoughts. I began to see that I was not alone in this struggle.

Many men hide their true selves beneath the demeanour of being macho, further digging their heels in.

I decided that enough was enough!

After completing my counselling sessions and gaining mental and emotional stability, I enrolled in a counselling course to qualify to help others. I took on personal responsibility to be the man who doesn't need to portray something that he isn't. I decided to undo all my social/cultural conditioning and reprogramme myself to live a healthier, happier, and more fulfilling life.

In 2015, a friend of mine gifted me a book called 'Emotional Intelligence' written by Daniel Goleman. I read a couple of chapters, but it just didn't interest me at the time. After going through my divorce, it was only later when I revisited this book, realising that it had all the answers I had been looking for. Since then, I have lived and breathed the principles stated in that book.

I went on to become a qualified Emotional Intelligence (EI) coach. This is where I realised things weren't right but could be corrected. Many times we don't need to do anything. EI teaches us acceptance and awareness and techniques to implement these.

I have accepted that my mum is gone and that it must have been painful for her. I have also accepted that the incident was a wake-up call for me. Had this not happened, I would still be on the hamster wheel. It was then I decided to honour my journey.

As I had discovered at the young age of 7, the reward was serving others, which became my lifesaver.

I found peace and satisfaction in doing so and my purpose. At the same time, I learned to speak at public events. I have delivered numerous youth and career events and have thoroughly enjoyed myself. I am mainly known as the Emotional Intelligence expert, who is out there to tear down social norms around a man's image.

I share my journey with people openly now hoping that it may become a survival guide for someone in need. I have been on a journey of personal development, counselling, and coaching. I coach people using EI and help them re-create their lives.

One quote that sums up all my learning is this:
"You are born to win but conditioned to Fail."

Speaking on international stages worldwide, working to empower youths and helping young people to pick the right career path has been a pleasure. I give out the message of Emotional Intelligence and its implication in all aspects of life. Being a renowned speaker and EI coach is an absolute pleasure; serving humanity is my goal.

I am a proud father of 3 young ladies. Being a dad is of utmost importance to me. What I do today is also my contribution to constructing and creating a better world for them. I wish to leave behind not just words and wealth but a legacy that would speak for itself.

The best advice I can give anyone today, after having lived for half a century on this earth, is that all you need to do to be happy is know yourself first. Denying your truth is not going to help you. Blocking your emotions rather than process and managing them will not do anyone a favour. You are valuable. Each human being is. We have massive value within us that we can offer to this world. This journey is not a competition. Whatever I can contribute to the world is still valuable; whatever you can is of enormous value too.

I understood and accepted this a few years ago.

When are you starting?

CHAPTER 14

Standing up for your Inner Superstar

By Sofia Nordgren

When I was three years old, I found myself sitting alone without my parents, on a plane travelling across half the globe from Bangladesh, my country of birth, to start a new life chapter in Sweden.

A couple adopted me in a small village outside Ludvika in Dalarna. My childhood proved challenging, with lots of fights within my adoptive family. School wasn't much better, and I experienced bullying in my early years. I started to write a diary about my experience as I wanted to share my experiences, but I was a little shy in my early childhood, so that would have to wait.

At my 9th grade graduation, I stood on the stage and read a poem I had written. I enjoyed the experience, and thankfully it was received well with appreciation. I sang as well with some other girls. My dreams of standing on an international stage as a public speaker culminated from this point.

I heard about the possibility of going to the United States as an exchange student, and a glimmer of hope ignited. I would have the opportunity to experience something very different. I created different ways to raise money to pay for the trip, and it finally happened. Once there, I gave my first international lecture sharing about Swedish culture and traditions. I loved it!

On my return to Sweden, I studied to become a registered nurse. This career kept me for 25 years within the health industry as a consultant and registered nurse with the bonus of working in over 100 different workplaces all over Sweden.

However, the work environment was very stressful with inefficient routines, low energy, low motivation, lack of passion, and many staff were also off sick. The advice we were to give patients I also felt was lacking. It was a highly frustrating unhealthy environment, and it had many adverse effects for me, but it proved to be a turning point.

I started to investigate how to educate and impact companies with a more holistic and sustainable health approach. My plan was forming.

After working in this environment for too long, I became sick and burned out. I found it difficult to sleep and focus, and I had anxiety. I asked for help at the healthcare clinic, and the doctor let me go home on sick leave, which I was on for several weeks. There was no advice on getting back on track, and there was no holistic or sustainable health advice or preventative care.

I started to educate myself more about health and began taking several different courses looking deeper into health, personal development, leadership, and business.

I decided to grab an opportunity for a public speaking course in London. With that, many other roles came my way, like becoming a Zumba instructor, a passion test coach and a stand-up comedian.

Then I created my healthcare formula on how to help companies, staff, managers, and entrepreneurs reach more sustainable and holistic health with my preventing care toolbox through inspirational speaking, individual coaching, and digital videos.

I did some health talks at some of my workplaces where I had been working as a nurse and current places I was still working as a nurse. I did my health talks three times for a health company on three different days. First, some theories about reaching optimum health through holistic methods, group exercises, meditation, and dance. The staff loved it and the manager who joined the dance exercise. I had tried my concept, and it worked, I asked for written and video testimonials, and they agreed.

I was part of an entrepreneurial network and heard they would have an event for female entrepreneurs. The audience was approximately 200 people and held at the high-class Sheraton hotel. I took the chance to apply my interest by sending them a short video. The keynote speakers were selected, but they allowed me to do a brief intro marketing talk for this international audience.

I remember practising a lot at home and outside. I'm lucky enough to live near the sea, so being in nature-inspired me. I remember speaking aloud whilst listening to the sea batter against the rocks.

The day came, and as my turn approached, I felt nervous and remembered the feeling was my own making, so I concentrated on getting focused and energised. I constantly get easily distracted by different sounds, so I practised techniques from my previous speaking courses.

The speech went very well, and I had terrific feedback from several people and the organiser.

I started to join a few Speaker agencies in Sweden to increase my number of new clients, but there is much competition out there, and agencies don't always get you the results as hoped. Some agencies prefer the more famous speakers who have been on TV or written a book.

I've joined various groups on social media to help me in my quest to find new and exciting speaking gigs. I also invest in speaking courses and recently attended one in Sweden, where the host was from the US. This has helped me improve my storytelling skills.

I decided to try a stand-up course for beginners, taking place in Stockholm. I was so nervous and had no idea how it worked or how I'd appear.

When I did my first stand-up-comedian performance, I had invited several of my friends, and there were around 100 people in the audience. I was shaking, but it turned out to be so much fun. I had hired a photographer to take some professional photos of me on stage, which I could add to my portfolio. It was a breathtaking experience on stage and tested my comfort zone!

I've continued doing stand-up shows during the years as I found a natural talent for it. It's is a harsh industry to get into, but I continue to do these shows, some for free and some paid to improve my skills.

An opportunity arose later on when I travelled to the US with my boyfriend, and I thought I would take the chance to watch other stand-up comedians whilst there in New

York. I mingled with the comedians at one of the shows to learn more about them. I was offered a stand-up gig at one of the men's clubs for the next day. I hesitated for a few seconds: I hadn't had time to practice in English yet, but I decided to say YES anyway! Unfortunately, my boyfriend didn't show me the support I needed and didn't want to attend the gig with me.

It was the first time I was in New York, and we travelled at the end of January. It was dark and cold, and the snow was on the streets. I couldn't find the way, and fear took over me. However, I pushed them aside, and my inner voice and passion guided me there. Once I arrived, I saw another girlfriend who I had invited show up, which boosted my confidence and made me happy.

Again, I was very nervous, but I had lots of laughs from the audience when it came to my turn. It was such a confidence boost, and I felt overwhelmed with joy. It was time to go home. I did two stand-up gigs, and they went very well; I am happy I had both recorded to remind me of all the fun moments on that trip.

I was at a smaller event in Stockholm where I met a woman who was the organiser of an international fashion show at City Hall. I wanted to join and had invited my then-boyfriend at that time. He was a lecturer and an author. The organiser asked for his phone number as I found out late, she wanted him to be a host. I wasn't even aware that she was looking for a moderator for the event. My boyfriend didn't consider mentioning my name to her, which made me angry as it would have been the perfect gig for me.

I called and informed the organiser of my skills as a lecturer and stand-up comedian. As a result, we both became moderators at City Hall for the International Fashion Week.

One lesson I learned was adapting to any given situation and creating and finding different solutions quickly, especially as these opportunities were presenting themselves.

I have now learned to work with good people and professional organisers who appreciate and thank me for the value and hard work I bring.

My latest work involves several online speeches for International Women's Day female networks. I practised speaking to over 250 people at a specific event, but the pandemic hit, and the event was cancelled. The good news is they still paid the speakers, which was great!

You learn so much when taking part in various speaking gigs, like how to set the right price for your time and always take into account the time it will also take you to write it, prepare and practice.

I was doing an online speech for a Swedish agency, and my theme and title was "Stand-up for your inner superstar" It is my common thread and is very much appreciated.

I created an opportunity to be part of two different TV shows in Sweden that included speaking, stand-up comedy and dancing skills. It was a great experience and a challenging one, but I learned so much.

I've had excellent feedback that people like to listen and get inspired, learn by my stories, experience, and speeches on how I face challenges, fear, find my passion and reach more holistic and sustainable health.

One of my motivations that has always driven me forward is to become an international speaker and a role model for others to inspire and educate on subjects close to my heart. I missed it myself during my upbringing to have successful female role models.

I cherish my experience, which has led me to be a moderator in City Hall, radio interviews, TV programs, stand-up comedy in New York, published in different magazines, book anthology and smaller roles in various TV shows/movies.

Sofia Nordgren is the CEO, Founder of Life+, Motivational speaker, Host, Co-author, Coach and a Stand-up-comedian!

She has been a host / moderator in the City Hall (where the Nobel prize is held), an international speaker and stand-up comedian in Berlin, New York and in Sweden. She has also appeared in Swedish TV-shows, a short movie and various magazines.

CHAPTER 15

Leaping from FEAR to FREEDOM

By Sue Curr

As I sat there shaking like the proverbial leaf waiting to be called to the podium once the current speaker had finished, my mind was frantically going over and over the opening words of my speech.

Willing myself get it right, not to stuff it up because even though I knew better, my inner critic was having a blessed birthday! Who do you think you are? People like you don't speak in public, etc. I knew I had to break the cycle to get back on track for fear of making a complete fool of myself.

Not for the first time, I was paralysed by the sort of fear-driven inaction, which, if we're not careful, not only steals our hopes and dreams but the promise of a brighter tomorrow too.

As if she knew what I was thinking, the speaker who was to follow me leaned over and whispered in my ear, "Are you ready for this, Sue?" It was the second time in 7 days that someone had used the exact words. Except on that occasion, my instructor leaned into me and said, " Are you ready for this, Sue?"

"Hell YES, let's get this party started, shall we?"

But this wasn't going to be any ordinary party. Nope, this particular 'party' was strictly a one-woman, two guys kinda gig taking place high above Hibaldstow in Lincolnshire. One which saw me at that point, securely attached to my tandem skydive instructor. We were sitting patiently at the open doorway of a small, light aircraft waiting for our signal to jump. I was in equal parts, monumentally excited and scared half to death as my legs dangled freely over the side.

Suddenly the cameraman who was going to film our jump launched himself clear of the plane and signalled for us to follow suit.

Almost before it even registered, my skydive partner launched us into the sixteen thousand feet of clean, fresh air which lay between us and the field below, wherein just a few short minutes, we'd land. Hopefully, in one piece!

In my mind, I was taking a leap of faith into sixteen thousand feet of fresh air to raise funds for MIND, the mental health charity, as part of a bigger quest to finally disempower my lifelong fear of heights so that I could authentically deem myself from that point on, to be 'truly fearless' and free myself from the shackles of a past that had long ago ceased to serve me.

I didn't know it then, but it was to become so much more than just doing a tandem skydive to raise funds for charity as a way of 'giving something back for the countless years of help and support I'd received whilst journeying along with life's loneliest of roads. That of mental ill-health.

It was to give me back my life and my voice!

I was 57 years old when I jumped and lived to tell the tale, but I'm not going to lie, during the initial sixty seconds of freefalling headfirst at a rate of 120 feet per second, I did, even though I was screaming 'FEARLESS' at the top of my lungs, think I was going to meet my maker.

I survived, and in doing so, it resulted in my experiencing a monumental paradigm shift, the like of which would come to mean I never, ever looked at life through a lens of fear again.

I didn't realise it at the time, but more than doing a skydive to raise funds for charity, I had finally made the leap from fear to freedom that I thought I'd made in 2012.

The difference was this time; I knew that I was ready to go all-in!

It wasn't an easy transition, but the first paradigm shift I'd experienced some five years previously had, in all honesty, paved the way and kickstarted my passion for fearing less and living a whole lot more, but it had come at a price.

During September 2012 and on the back of a life-long journey with mental ill-health. One which had reached the point where it had unravelled into full-blown, near-fatal alcoholism. I was admitted to the hospital as an emergency; with end-stage liver failure, my doctors began the seemingly impossible task of both stabilising my condition and trying to save my life.

It was a battle I almost lost several times, and my family were repeatedly told to prepare for the worst. Slowly but surely, I began to stabilise as I began to respond to treatment, but I knew I was far from out of the woods when my consultant came to see me one afternoon and delivered his verdict…

"You've won the battle but not the war Susan; I'm sorry to tell you, you're still dying!"

At that point, paradigm shift number two kicked in, and I was suddenly aware that I was promising myself that even though I didn't know if, let alone how I'd get out of there alive, I did know that if I did, things would change for the better, forever.

Not only was it time to wake up and smell the coffee instead of the Chardonnay. It was time to take responsibility for a life that was mine alone to live, including the 'story I'd been telling myself about how and why I'd ended up in this mess to start with.

It had been a long time coming, but it was, shall we say, simultaneously the final curtain coming down on my 'old life' and the opening night of my new one.

For fifty-two years until that point, my 'old life' had been lived on the rocky foundations of familiar and environmental learned belief and behaviour patterns.

They were patterns that saw me grow into a people pleaser, someone who by the time she'd reached adulthood was routinely saying yes to the demands and expectations of others when no would have been a far, far more sensible option. Someone who, although she had much to say, had learned at a very early age to sit still, be quiet and do as I was told.

By the time I was five, I'd learned a hell of a lot!

I knew how to laugh but had learned how to cry.

I knew how to shine but had learned how to hide.

I knew how to be happy but had learned how to be sad.

I knew how to play but had learned how to sit.

I knew how to be real but had learned how to be fake.

I knew how to speak but had learned how to be silent.

I adapted very quickly to the circumstances of our family life. It's fair to say that I'd been moulded (albeit unwittingly) into an outwardly confident but inwardly timid, insecure, anxious people pleaser.

I'd learned how to behave for fear of doing something wrong or being seen to be lacking in some way and grew up feeling stupid, worthless, but most of all unlovable.

I'd learned to speak when I was spoken to!

But by the time I was fifty-seven and sat with my legs dangling in sixteen thousand feet of fresh air, I'd not only learned; I knew a whole lot more than I did when I was five.

I knew how to cry but had remembered how to laugh.

I knew how to hide but had remembered how to shine.

I knew how to be sad but had remembered how to be happy.

I knew how to sit but had remembered how to play.

I knew how to be fake but had remembered how to be real.

I knew how to be silent but had remembered how to speak.

For sure, my old life had seen me emotionally, mentally, and spiritually bereft. Simply because I hadn't known any better, but in the final few moments before I jumped, I suddenly realised not only was I trusting that my instructor would guide us safely to the ground, but I was also trusting the process. Moreover, for the first time in forever, I was not only trusting that I'd made the right decision, I believed that I could do it.

In that split second, I knew beyond doubt that my self-belief was giving me the wings to fly, the courage to fall and the confidence to get back up to do it (and anything else I put my mind to from that point on) all over again if I chose to do so.

Suddenly I was brought back to reality as I heard the words.

'Five, four, three, two, one .... go' .... and we jumped!

Bar none, the experience was the best of times, the worst of times, the most exhilarating time of my life to date. It taught me more about myself and what I could do, be and become within the realms of my own life than anything else ever had.

A life that in the moment I landed, I knew without a shadow of a doubt that from that point on, I was going to live in my way, on my terms. Whilst basking in the glorious technicolour reflection of life, I would forever see through a lens of opportunity instead of one full of fear.

Such was the shift I'd experienced in the brief window of time it took to land safely on the ground.

"Sue, Sue, are you listening? You're on."

Suddenly I was no longer on the edge of a light aircraft preparing to launch myself into sixteen thousand feet of fresh air, nor even in the field below having made the jump.

I was back in the room at The World Forum Centre in The Hague, being called to the podium to deliver my first-ever speech to a packed, multi-international audience.

As if that weren't pressure enough. I was following on from Kruti Parek, India's most famous female mentalist (think 10x Derren Brown), and this time my knees, along with the rest of my body, including my voice, were shaking for real. Sensing my nerves, my co-speaker squeezed my hand and gave me an encouraging smile as the host took to the stage, and in the loudest voice, I'd ever heard announced.

'Ladies and gentlemen, please welcome our next speaker, Ms Sue Curr, from the United Kingdom.'

Praying silently that my legs wouldn't give way and I wouldn't fall flat on my face, I stood up, walked slowly and deliberately to centre stage, took a deep breath and readied myself for my debut speech.

There was an eerie silence as I paused and allowed myself to scan the faces of the audience before me. Suddenly I was filled with a sense of knowing everything that had gone before. Everything that had ever happened to me had served to bring me to that point in time.

It was where I was meant to be before the world had taught me otherwise, and for the first time in a very long time, I started to speak safely in the knowledge that my audience was listening.

I had gained my wings.

I'd reclaimed my life.

"'Good afternoon everyone, George Benson penned the words ''learning to love ourselves is the greatest love of all'', once I believed that, my life changed for the better forever. Yet just five short years ago, I was down, depressed, drunk, and quite literally almost dead.

Today I'm blessed to use the voice I was gifted to empower others to understand that it doesn't have to be like that.

My name is Sue Curr, and I'm here to take you on a journey from fear to freedom.

The rest, as they say, is history…

Epilogue

Thank you for purchasing a copy of this book.

I hope you were able to find some answers to your own situation or take some knowledge away to use in your own life.

The Authors within these pages have dedicated their career to finding the answers on areas they are passionate about and are dedicated to sharing those life lessons with their audiences.

If you would like to share your own experience, please do contact us for details on how you can take part in our next book.

If you enjoyed this book, we would love a review on Amazon.

About the Creator

Sharon Brown moved to the West Midlands in 2003 from Glasgow in Scotland. After a wide-ranging career in Event Management, Marketing, Project Management and board level support in various different industries, Sharon's passion around organising events led her to launch Lydian Events Ltd in 2015 whilst still working full time.

In 2017 Sharon took the plunge and left her corporate position to move into Self-employment full time. It wasn't long after this that Sharon soon realised the way business was heading and decided to launch an online platform for women in business in 2018 called Revival Sanctuary. The aim of this was connecting women globally in order to find collaborative projects to work together and build each other up.

In 2021, Sharon changed the name of her business to Lydian Group Ltd which supports four online platforms through writing, speaking, publishing and community opportunities.

Services

MO2VATE Magazine | The Winning Formula

mo2vatemagazine.com | editor@mo2vatemagazine.com

A global publication which highlights the writing ability and knowledge around business, health and inspirational stories of small business owners the world over.

———

THE BOOK CHIEF | Ignite Your Writing

Thebookchief.com | sharon@thebookchief.com

An affordable and full service to get your manuscript edited, typeset and published through a recognised brand with a niche in collaborative books.

———

THE SPEAKERS INDEX | Amplify Your Voice

Thespeakersindex.com | sharon@thespeakersindex.com

A speakers and event organiser directory and magazine to allow you to get in front of the right people.

———

REVIVAL SANCTUARY | Women in business

Revivalsanctuary.co.uk | sharon@revivalsanctuary.co.uk

Exclusive Private Membership Club for women in business. It attracts women who are comfortable in their own skin, supportive of other women and those willing to empower and collaborate with each other.

———

Printed in Great Britain
by Amazon